TinkerActive

WORKBOOKS

1ST GRADE · ENGLISH LANGUAGE ARTS · AGES 6–7

by Megan Hewes Butler

illustrated by Taryn Johnson

educational consulting by Mindy Yip

 Odd Dot · New York

The Alphabet

A **fictional text** describes imaginary events and people. With the help of an adult, read this fiction story aloud.

The Tag Sale

Honk, honk! Today was Brian and Amelia's tag sale. Amelia squeezed her old bicycle horn to let all the neighbors know. Brian hung a big sign in his front yard. Amelia put price tags on a drum and a sled. Brian put price tags on a bat, a sock, and a toy ship.

Soon their neighbors arrived. Brian's friend Zed bought a flag for his tree house for one dollar. Amelia's teacher bought a toy car tire for twenty-five cents.

At the end of the day, Brian and Amelia had sold everything! They counted the money—they had earned ten dollars and thirty cents! Amelia wanted to throw an ice cream party. Brian wanted a new swing.

In the end, they agreed to give the money to Tinker Town's animal shelter. When they went to the shelter with their donation, Amelia and Brian got to play with all the animals!

Draw a line to lead Amelia and Brian to the animal shelter. Start at A and follow the letters in alphabetical order to Z. Trace each letter as you go.

A B C D E

I

F

P M L K J I H G L

N

K

O P Q R S T W

R

U

S W V

T X Y

Y

Z

A, E, I, O, and U are vowels. Circle the vowels.

Write each missing uppercase letter.

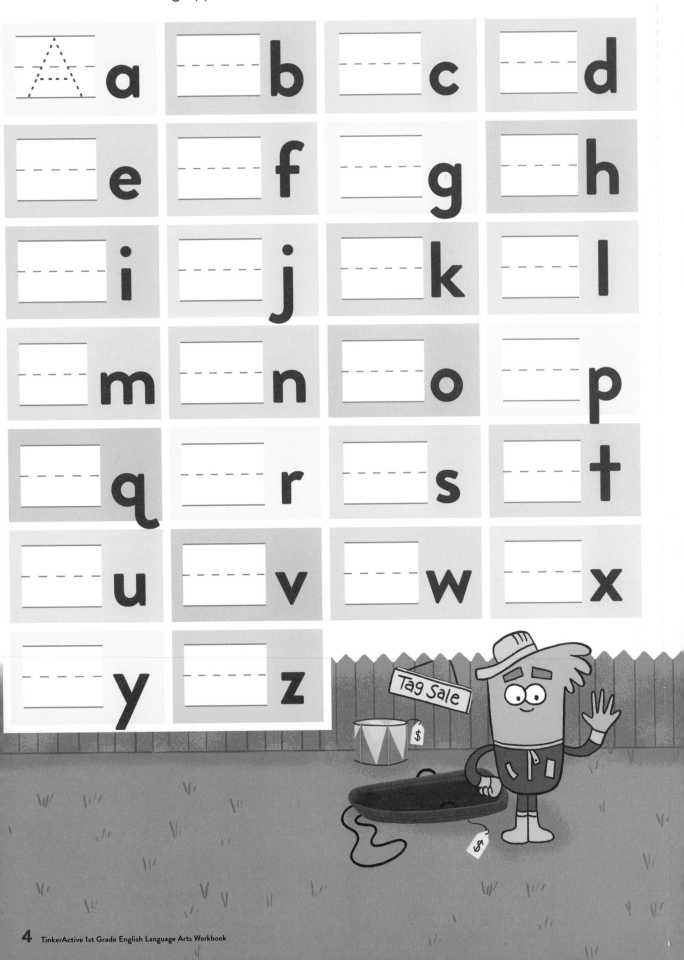

a b c d

e f g h

i j k l

m n o p

q r s t

u v w x

y z

Write each missing lowercase letter.

A a   B ___   C ___

D ___   E ___   F ___   G ___

H ___   I ___   J ___   K ___

L ___   M ___   N ___   O ___

P ___   Q ___   R ___   S ___

T ___   U ___   V ___   W ___

X ___   Y ___   Z ___

Vowels can make different sounds. **Long vowels** sound just like their names—like the e's in bee!

Read each word with a long vowel sound aloud. Then circle the other objects with long vowels.

cage | lace | bat | paint

bee | pen | leaf | wheel

bike | tire | pie | ship

rose | coat | lock | bow

glue | mug | tube | flute

Short vowels make a different sound—they don't sound like their names.

Read each word with a short vowel sound aloud. Then circle the objects with short vowels.

m**a**p

flag

clay

fan

n**e**t

teeth

bell

sled

w**i**g

dish

dice

bin

s**o**ck

bone

mop

frog

c**u**p

bus

drum

cube

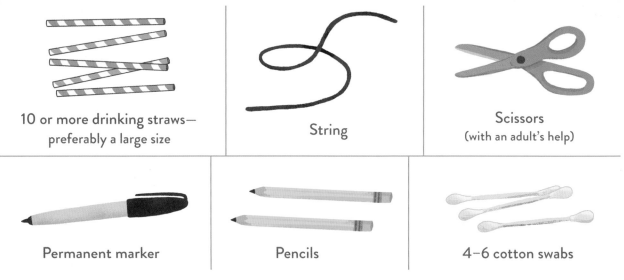

10 or more drinking straws—preferably a large size

String

Scissors (with an adult's help)

Permanent marker

Pencils

4–6 cotton swabs

LET'S TINKER!

Make the shape of the capital letter A with your materials. Next, **try** B. How many letters of the alphabet can you make? Can you make uppercase and lowercase letters? Can you spell your name?

LET'S MAKE: ALPHABET GAME!

1. **Cut** drinking straws into pieces about the length of your thumb. **Make** 26 pieces.

2. **Flatten** one straw piece and write the letter A on it with a permanent marker. **Write** the letter B on another piece. **Keep going** until you've written the entire alphabet.

3. Thread the straws onto a piece of string in alphabetical order, starting with A.

4. When all 26 are on, **cut** the string and tie the ends into a knot to make a loop.

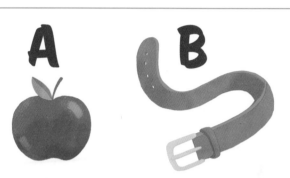

5. Starting with A, **find** an object in your home that starts with that letter: like an apple or your ankle! Then **slide** to the next letter on the string: B. **Find** an object in your home that starts with every letter of the alphabet! How many rounds can you complete without repeating objects?

LET'S ENGINEER!

Callie is having her own tag sale. She has two tables: a short vowel table and a long vowel table. So far, the short vowel table is empty.

How can she make some items with short vowels for her tag sale?

Use your materials to make items with short vowels. Can you make a wig or a ring? What about a map or a hat? What other short vowel items can you make?

PROJECT 1: DONE!
Get your sticker!

A **limerick** is a poem that has five lines that rhyme in a pattern and is funny. With the help of an adult, read the limerick, written by Edward Lear, aloud. Then answer the questions.

There Was an Old Man with a Beard

There was an old man with a beard,

Who said, "It is just as I feared,

Two owls and a hen,

A lark and a wren,

Have all built their nests in my beard!"

Which word rhymes with **beard**?

_____

- - - - - - - - - - - - - - -

_____

Which word rhymes with **hen**?

_____

- - - - - - - - - - - - - - -

_____

What is another word you know that rhymes with **hen**?

WHENGEN

Say the sound of each letter. Then read the name of each bird. Last, trace each word.

jay   gull   crane

duck   tern   crow

Make up your own bird that has made a nest in this beard. Draw a picture and write its name.

The name of my bird is

With the help of an adult, read the limerick, written by Edward Lear, aloud.

There Was an Old Man Who Supposed

There was an old man who supposed

That the street door was partially closed;

But some very large rats

Ate his coats and his hats,

While that futile old gentleman dozed.

Which words rhyme with **supposed**?

_____   _____

- - - - - - - - - - - -   - - - - - - - - - - - -

_____   _____

Which word rhymes with **rats**?

_____

- - - - - - - - - - - -

_____

What is another word you know that rhymes with **rats**?

_____

- - - - - - - - - - - -

_____

Act it out! What did the rats do when they snuck in the door?

A **syllable** is a word, or part of a word, that is pronounced as one beat.

These words have one syllable. Read each word aloud and clap once for the one syllable.

coat

hat

These words have two syllables. Read each word aloud and clap twice for the two syllables.

zipper

swimsuit

Read the name of each object aloud and clap for each syllable. Circle the objects that have only one syllable.

necklace

vest

ring

pajamas

dress

rat

scarf

In some words, two consonants work together to make one sound. This is called a **digraph**.

Read each word aloud. Listen to how each digraph forms one sound. Then draw a line to match each word to the correct picture.

shoes   **sh**irt   **sh**orts   **sh**ovel

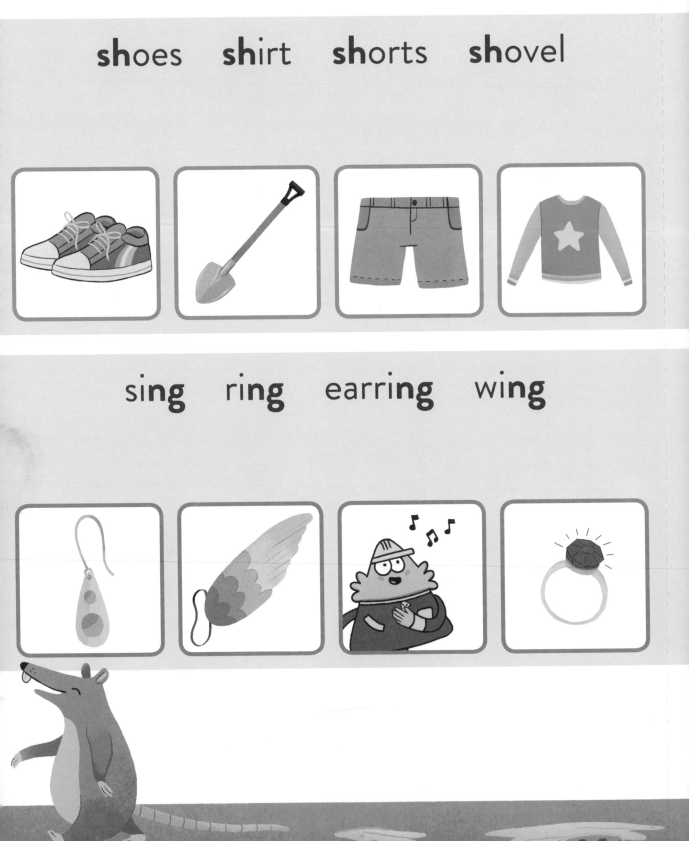

si**ng**   ri**ng**   earri**ng**   wi**ng**

In some words, two consonants work together, but each individual sound can still be heard. This is called a **blend**.

Read each word aloud. Listen to how each blend has two sounds. Then draw a line to match each word to the correct picture.

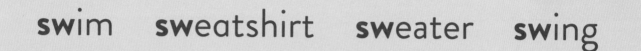

swim   **sw**eatshirt   **sw**eater   **sw**ing

shi**rt**   di**rt**   ski**rt**   hea**rt**

LET'S START! GATHER THESE TOOLS AND MATERIALS.

Thick paper or cardboard	Markers	Newspaper	Cup	Food coloring	Tablespoon
Spoon	4–6 drinking straws	Pencil	6 or more rubber bands	6 or more twist ties	Tissues

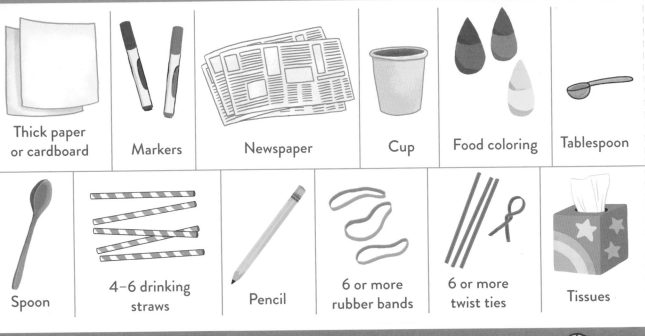

LET'S TINKER!

Hunt for items with one-syllable names, like a pen and a hat. **Look** around your home or find items in your materials. **Clap** to make sure that each item you pick has only one syllable!

bag

pot

LET'S MAKE: BEARD NESTS!

1. Draw a face on a thick sheet of paper, like watercolor paper or cardboard.

2. Lay it on top of a piece of newspaper. This can get messy!

3. Mix 3 drops of one color of food coloring and 1 tablespoon of water in a cup.

4. Use a spoon to add one drop of the colored water to the bottom of the face drawing.

5. Blow through a straw to spread the water and create a beard.

6. You can **try** again with the same color or mix a new color in another cup.

7. When the water is dry, **use** a pencil to add birds to your beard.

LET'S ENGINEER!

Some birds near Dimitri's home don't have a nest. So he wants to build one for them! The problem is that every time he builds one, it falls apart when he lifts it onto a tree branch.

How can he build a nest that won't fall apart when he picks it up?

Use your materials to make a nest. **Test** it by picking it up—does it fall apart or stay together? Which materials work best? As you work, **say** the name of each material you use aloud. Which letter sound does each begin with? Which letter sound does each end with?

PROJECT 2: DONE!
Get your sticker!

Word Building

A **legend** is an old story that has been shared for a long time. Parts of the story may be true, but no one knows for sure. With the help of an adult, read the legend aloud.

Johnny Appleseed

John Chapman was an apple farmer who was born in 1774. As a young man, he traveled the country. He dreamed of planting enough apple trees so that no one would go hungry. There would be apples for everyone in the whole country.

The legend says that John lived outside. He slept on the ground and walked barefoot. He may have worn a scratchy burlap sack for clothes and a cooking pot as a hat! He also carried a leather bag everywhere he went.

John visited mills that made apple cider. He would ask for their extra apple seeds and put them in his bag. As he wandered, he spread apple seeds and returned later to care for the apple trees that had grown.

John met lots of people and made many friends. People called him Johnny Appleseed because of his love for apples. He spread seeds for over fifty years and planted thousands of trees!

Prefixes and suffixes are groups of letters that can be added to a word to make a new word. Knowing prefixes and suffixes can help you figure out unknown words.

Prefixes go at the start of words.	
re- means again	**un-** means not
refill with water means to fill again with water	**uneven row** means a row that is not even

Suffixes go at the end of words.	
-ful means full of	**-less** means without
colorful apples means apples full of color	**seedless grapes** means grapes without seeds

Circle the picture that matches each phrase.

feeling unhappy

painful sting

repainted sign

feeling cheerful

unripe apple

toothless animal

Inflectional endings can be added to the end of words to change their meanings.

-s or **-es** means more than one	**-ing** means an action is happening now	**-ed** means an action happened in the past
seed**s**	plant**ing**	plant**ed**

Write the inflectional ending for each word.

add **s**

shovel ____

add **ing**

water ____

add **ed**

pick ____

bag ____

fall ____

fix ____

apple ____

eat ____

climb ____

A **root word** is a word without any inflectional endings, prefixes, or suffixes.

plant

plants planting planted replant

Read each word aloud and circle the root word.

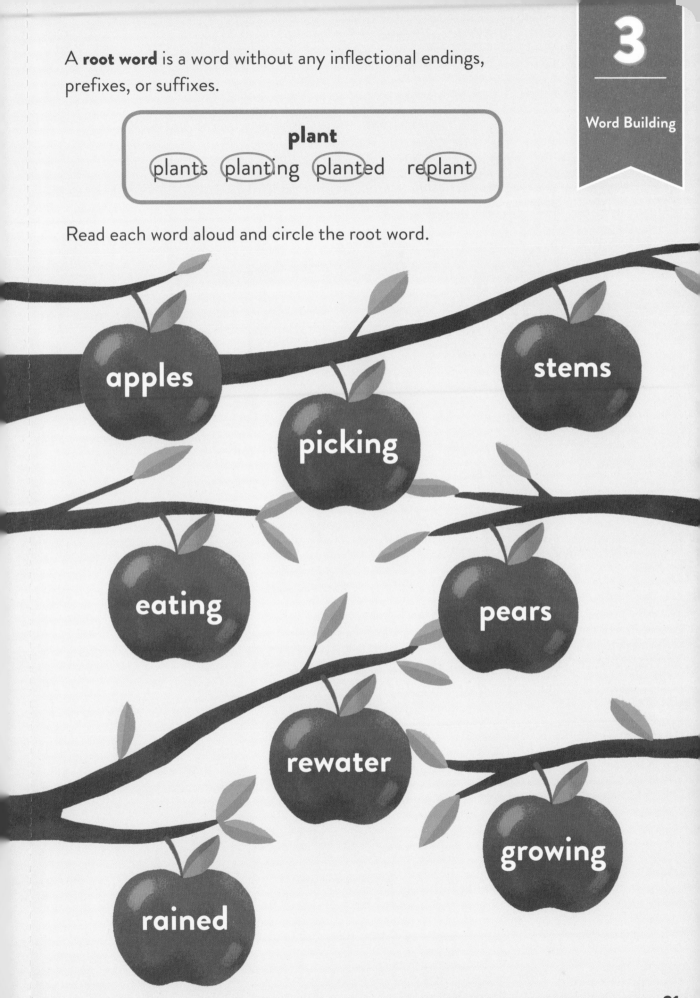

apples

picking

stems

eating

pears

rewater

growing

rained

When a word ends with a silent **e**, the vowel in front of it usually makes a long vowel sound.

rake kite same

When two vowels are next to each other, the first one usually makes a long vowel sound.

rain fruit pie

Draw a line through the apple orchard that only passes words with long vowel sounds.

LET'S START! GATHER THESE TOOLS AND MATERIALS.

2–3 apples	Paint	Paper plate	Paper

Cardboard (from a shipping box or cereal box)	Scissors (with an adult's help)	Markers

LET'S TINKER!

Move your materials according to these verbs:

> bend stack poke roll push

Add re- to these verbs to move your materials again. For example: rebend means to bend again. Then **move** your materials with your own verbs!

LET'S MAKE: APPLE AND SEED PRINTS!

1. With the help of an adult, **cut** the apples in half—some lengthwise and some widthwise.

2. Pour paint onto a paper plate.

3. Press the cut side of an apple into the paint.

4. Press the apple onto your paper.

5. Lift it up. What shape did each make?

6. Press more apple shapes into your paper to make your own design.

LET'S ENGINEER!

The MotMots made their own word-building game! They put together root words and endings to make word sculptures. Whoever can make the most words wins!

How can each MotMot make as many word sculptures as possible?

Build your own word sculptures. With the help of an adult, **cut** twelve rectangles about the size of your hand from a piece of cardboard. Then **make** four small V-shaped cuts in each one. **Use** four of the rectangles to write each of the following endings:

> **-s   -es   -ing   -ed**

Now, **write** your root words on the remaining rectangles. **Think** about the things you like to do, such as play or read. What happens when you put the endings on those root words? You can **make** "plays" or "reading." Last, **build** a sculpture with the rectangles. How many words can you make? How big can you make your sculpture?

PROJECT 3: DONE!
Get your sticker!

Vocabulary

A **letter** is a written message. With the help of an adult, read the letters aloud.

Dear Ava,

We hope this letter gets to you in Alaska. Is it cold there all the time? Is your new home on an iceberg? Do you ride a dog sled to get to school?

We miss you!

Sincerely,

Ms. Tinkerton's Class

Dear Ms. Tinkerton's class,

Hello from Alaska! It is not cold all the time. During the winter it is dark, cold, and snowy. But during the summer it is warm and sunny. Sometimes I can even wear shorts!

My home is not on an iceberg—it's on green grass. There is some ice in Alaska, but there are also swamps, forests, and mountains.

I ride a yellow school bus to get to school. There are roads and cars just like in Tinker Town. I see a lot of moose out the window. They are everywhere!

I miss you too!

Sincerely,

Your friend Ava

Circle the person the class wrote a letter to.

Ava

Ms. Tinkerton

Circle the habitats Ava can see in Alaska.

swamp

mountains

desert

How does Ava get to school? _____

Circle what Ava might wear in the summer.

A **pronoun** is a word that takes the place of a noun.

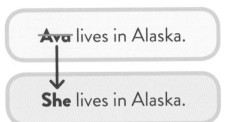

~~Ava~~ lives in Alaska.

↓

She lives in Alaska.

Fill in the correct pronoun to complete each sentence.

She Her

_____ got new warm boots.

They Them

_____ like to write.

Me I

_____ saw a moose.

Us We

_____ miss Ava.

A **determiner** is a word that comes before a noun and gives more information about what the noun is referring to.

A bus was late.   **This** bus was late.

Two buses were late.

Write the correct determiner to complete each sentence.

a   an

Ava wore _____ sunhat.

This   These

_____ is an iceberg.

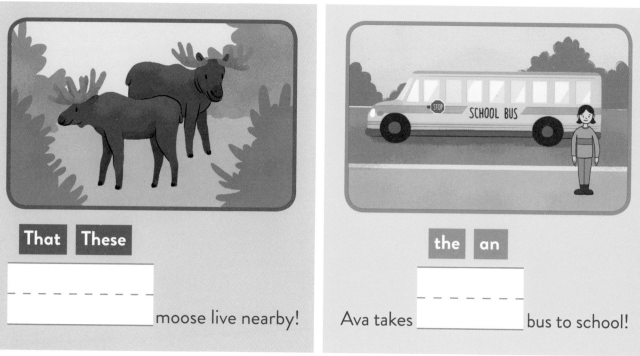

That   These

_____ moose live nearby!

the   an

Ava takes _____ bus to school!

Write the correct determiner to describe each of Ava's photographs.

one   two   three   four

sun

mountains

buses

moose

icebergs

school

Write your own letter to a friend.

Dear _____,

I live in _____. My home is _____

_____.

To get to school I _____.

Here, the weather is _____. I like to wear

_____ and _____.

There are animals near me, too. I see _____ all

the time! My favorite animal to see is _____.

It is very _____. What I like the most about

living here is _____.

Sincerely,

_____

Copy your letter onto a separate piece of
paper and mail it with the help of an adult.

LET'S START! GATHER THESE TOOLS AND MATERIALS.

Items from outside your home, like:
leaves, twigs, flowers, seeds, pinecones

Paper

Glue

Pencil

Markers

Shoebox

Scissors
(with an adult's help)

LET'S TINKER!

What clothes did you wear today for the weather where you live? **Use** the materials to make drawings or models of what you wore. **Describe** each item with pronouns. **Try** using "it," "they," and "them." What color are they? How many do you have? **Use** color and number words to describe your materials.

LET'S MAKE: COMMUNITY COLLAGE!

1. Gather the items from outside your home.

2. Place the materials onto a piece of paper. **Create** a design that shows something about the place where you live. **Lay** things in rows, in shapes, stacked together, or however you would like.

3. Glue the materials onto the paper once you have an arrangement you like!

What kind of leaves and flowers did you collect? What could grow from the seeds? Do you know the name of each material? If not, **ask** an adult to help you find out about the trees, flowers, and other items in nature near where you live.

LET'S ENGINEER!

A new family just moved into Tinker Town. Callie wants to tell them all about it, but they speak a different language!

How can Callie share details about Tinker Town if she can't talk about it?

Make a diorama in a shoebox about the place where you live to share with a friend or family member. A diorama is a model. It can show what your neighborhood looks like. **Label** important things in your diorama that you want to share.

my HOME

PROJECT 4: DONE!
Get your sticker!

A **flyer** is a piece of paper with information about an event, a person, a place, or a thing. Read the flyer aloud.

Prepositions are words that can describe where something is located or when something happens.

Read each question and circle the correct answer.

What will happen **before** the Doughnut Race?

| 🚩 Doughnut Parade | 🎺 Concert | 🎭 Costume Contest |

What will happen **next to** the concert in the park?

| 🏆 Doughnut Race | 🎭 Costume Contest | 🛡 Police Ball |

What will the MotMots pass during the parade?

Where will the parade end?

| in the park | outside the park |

What can the MotMots do **after** the concert?

| 🚩 Doughnut Parade | 🎺 Concert | 🎭 Costume Contest |

An **adjective** is a word that describes a person, place, or thing. Adjectives can describe color, shape, size, and more!

Circle the adjective that describes each doughnut.

red   blue

square   round

whole   broken

fancy   plain

flat   tall

tiny   large

Write the adjective that describes each doughnut.

hot   mushy   small

Cross out the words that are not adjectives.

colorful
eat
large
sweet
napkin
fresh
yummy
parade

Draw your own doughnut. Then write four adjectives to describe it.

Draw a line to connect each MotMot to the adjective that describes his costume.

silly   fancy   sparkling

Draw your own costume for the Doughnut Parade. Then write three adjectives to describe it.

_____   _____   _____

_____   _____   _____

You can be in the Doughnut Parade, too!
Read each action word, and then act it out.

walk   **march**   **stomp**

skip   **stroll**

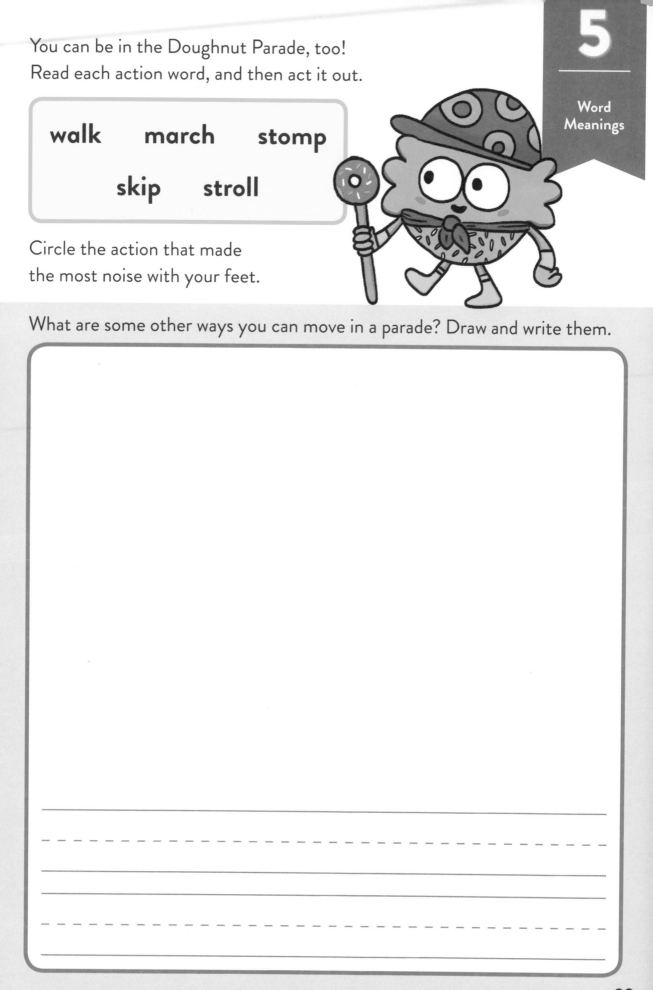

Circle the action that made
the most noise with your feet.

What are some other ways you can move in a parade? Draw and write them.

LET'S START! GATHER THESE TOOLS AND MATERIALS.

Empty tissue box	Construction paper	Paper	Glue
Paint	Scissors (with an adult's help)	Markers	

LET'S TINKER!

Find a partner and lay all the materials in front of you. Secretly **choose** a material and describe it to your partner using only adjectives, like descriptions of color, shape, or size. For example, you can say, "I see something red and smooth and flat," to describe red paper. Can your partner guess which object you chose? **Take** turns describing and guessing.

LET'S MAKE: WIGGLE BOX!

1. **Decorate** an empty tissue box. You can **use** markers, paper, glue, paint, and more.

2. **Cut** a sheet of paper into 10 pieces.

3. Write an action word on each piece, such as hop, wiggle, gallop, or roar. Then **put** all 10 in the box.

4. Find a partner to play. **Pull** one word from the box and read it aloud. Then **do** the action. For example, if you pull "wiggle," then you wiggle!

5. Next, your partner **pulls** out a word and reads it. He or she must **do** both actions in order. For example, if your partner pulls out "gallop," first he or she must wiggle, then gallop.

6. Keep going to see who can do the most actions in a row!

LET'S ENGINEER!

The MotMots are throwing a pajama parade and inviting lots of friends.

How can they show or tell their friends where the parade will be?

Make your own pajama parade route and instructions. Will the parade go through your bedroom? Will it start next to your dog's bed? How will you show or tell your friends where it starts and ends?

PROJECT 5: DONE!
Get your sticker!

Working with Unknown Words

An **essay** is a piece of writing about one specific topic. With the help of an adult, read the essay aloud.

The Flute

I learned to play a new instrument—the flute! It is my favorite instrument. The flute makes a pretty whistling sound. It is called a wind instrument because you can make sounds by blowing air through it.

The flute has three important parts. There is a lip plate at the top. You put your mouth on the lip plate and blow air across a hole. The body of the flute is a long, hollow tube. It is empty inside so it can carry air to the keys. The keys are small metal parts that cover the holes in the body. Each one has a hinge. You can swing them open and closed by pressing with your fingers. That's how you change the sound that comes out of the flute!

The flute is my favorite musical instrument. It is the best because it hums and whistles. I keep mine close to my bed at night. I can't wait to play it again.

Circle the words in the essay that are new to you.

The author wrote that the flute is hollow—it is empty inside.
Circle the object below that is hollow.

Flute keys each have a hinge—you can swing them open and closed.
Circle the object below that has a hinge.

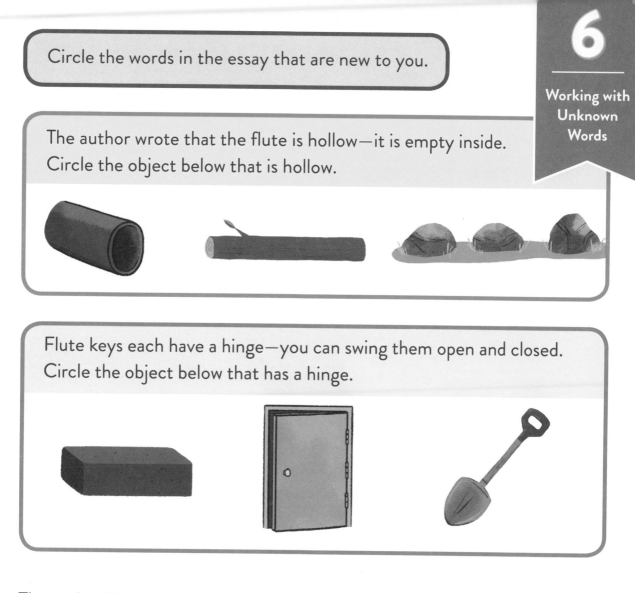

The author likes the flute's whistling sound. The sound is made by blowing
air. Draw a picture of something else that makes a whistling sound.

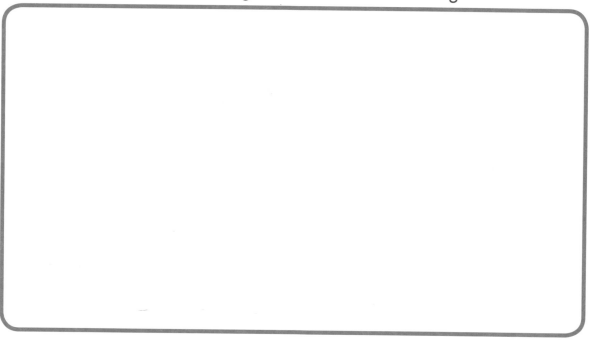

Read each sentence and look at the underlined word. Then circle the word below the sentence that means the same thing.

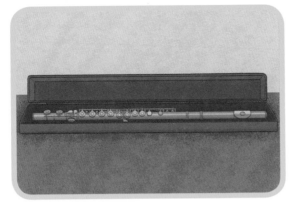

The skinny flute fit into a narrow case.

thin   thick

I heard a distant sound from the flute player down the street.

close   far

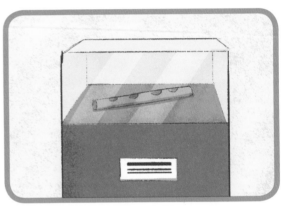

I saw an ancient flute made from a bone in a museum.

old   new

The mellow music made me sleepy.

soft   loud

No one else was on stage—I played solo.

together   alone

A **homograph** is a word that is spelled like another word but that is different in meaning.

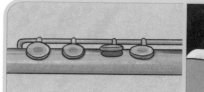

The flute keys open and **close**.

Frank keeps his flute **close** to his bed.

Frank's flute is not heavy. It's **light**.

Circle another meaning of **light**.

Frank hears the bell **ring** at the end of school.

Circle another meaning of **ring**.

Frank **waves** to his flute teacher.

Circle another meaning of **waves**.

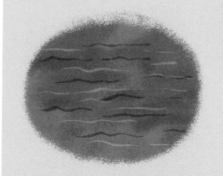

A **conjunction** is a word that joins together two words or phrases. Fill in the missing conjunction to complete each sentence.

Music class is fun _____ we play instruments.

because   **or**

I tried the trumpet _____ it was hard to play.

but   **or**

Today I played the flute _____ I tried the drums!

because   **and**

I want to play the banjo _____ sing in a band.

or   **so**

I like wind instruments _____ I am learning the flute.

or   **so**

Complete each sentence.

Dimitri likes to play his sitar alone **but**

_____

_____

_____.

Enid's tuba is big **so** _____

_____

_____

_____.

Amelia can't play her bongos **because**

_____

_____

_____.

LET'S START! GATHER THESE TOOLS AND MATERIALS.

Jar with a lid

4–6 rubber bands

Tape

4–6 craft sticks

10 or more drinking straws

2 thick books

LET'S TINKER!

Use your materials to make sounds. **Try** tapping, folding, and rubbing them. Can you make sounds like these?

> click   buzz   snap

What are other words that describe the sounds you hear?

LET'S MAKE: TINY BANJO!

1. Wrap 4 thin rubber bands around a jar lid. (If the rubber bands are loose, you can **wrap** them around twice so they are tighter.)

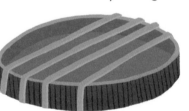

2. Tape them down on the flat back.

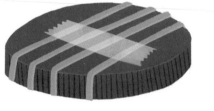

3. Tape a craft stick to the flat back as a handle.

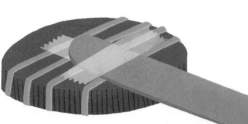

4. Pluck the strings
to make music.
Describe the
sounds you make!
And **sing** along!

LET'S ENGINEER!

The MotMots took a shortcut to the playground, and there is a river they can't
get across! But Enid realizes that a bridge works just like a conjunction—it joins
together two places!

How can they build a bridge over the river to get to the playground?

Place two thick books on a table and leave room for your hand in between
them. Then **make** a bridge using your materials. Can you get it to go from
one book to the other? **Try** making a bigger space between the books, enough
for two hands. How long can you make your bridge between the books?

PROJECT 6: DONE!
Get your sticker!

Reading Literature

A **fairy tale** is a story about magical characters, settings, and events that aren't real. With the help of an adult, read this fairy tale aloud.

Jack and the Beanstalk

Once upon a time a boy named Jack lived in a cottage with his mother. They needed money for food, so Jack's mother told him to sell their only cow. On the way to town Jack ran into an old man. "I will trade you your old cow for five magic beans!" the man said. Jack took the magic beans and ran home proudly. But instead of being happy, his mother was angry. She turned bright red and said, "Now we have only five beans and no cow!" Then she threw the beans out the window.

Overnight the beans grew and grew and grew. When Jack awoke, the beanstalk reached the sky! He jumped out of bed and started climbing the beanstalk. He climbed above his cottage and above the clouds, and he saw a shimmering castle. Inside he saw gold coins all around.

Suddenly a giant came into the room. He boomed, "Fee-fi-fo-fum! I see you, you better run!" Jack started running. The giant chased him around the castle! But Jack was too fast for the giant. He hid and the giant sat down and took a nap. Jack quietly grabbed a bag of gold coins and climbed down the beanstalk. He gave the coins to his mother, and she was happy.

Later on, Jack and his mother needed more money for food. So Jack climbed the beanstalk and went to the castle. The giant was there, napping again. Jack grabbed a

magical goose and a golden harp. He began to climb down the beanstalk, but the harp made a noise. The giant woke up and boomed, "Fee-fi-fo-fum! I see you, you better run!" Jack climbed down as fast as he could. The giant chased him down the beanstalk, but Jack was still too fast. He jumped to the ground, grabbed an ax, and chopped down the beanstalk. The giant fell to the ground, and the beanstalk fell on top of him. Jack and his mother lived happily ever after.

The end.

What did Jack trade to get the magic beans?

_____

Circle the picture of how Jack's mother felt when he brought home beans.

Circle all the items Jack took from the castle.

What did Jack do with the ax? _____

_____

Stories like fairy tales have settings, characters, and events.

A **setting** is a place in a story.

Draw a picture of what you think these settings may have looked like.

the cottage

the castle

A **character** is a person or animal in a story.

Draw a picture of what you think these characters may have looked like.

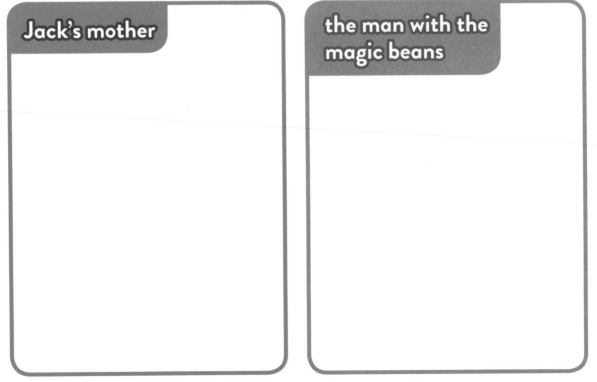

Jack's mother

the man with the magic beans

Jack

the giant

Circle two adjectives
that describe Jack.

fast   **small**

angry   **giant**

Circle two adjectives
that describe the giant.

large   **happy**

sleepy   **tiny**

Complete the sentence.

Jack climbed up the beanstalk

because _____

_____

_____ .

Complete the sentence.

The giant climbed down the

beanstalk because _____

_____

_____ .

Write how each character may have felt during each event in the story.
Then act out the events!

proud **angry**

Jack feels

_____.

Jack's mother feels

_____.

mad **scared**

Jack feels

_____.

The giant feels

_____.

worried **confident**

Jack feels

_____.

The giant feels

_____.

Write the numbers 1, 2, 3, 4, and 5 to put these events from "Jack and the Beanstalk" in order from first to last.

LET'S START! GATHER THESE TOOLS AND MATERIALS.

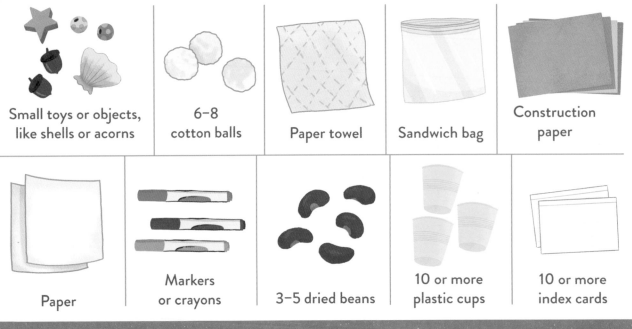

Small toys or objects, like shells or acorns	6–8 cotton balls	Paper towel	Sandwich bag	Construction paper
Paper	Markers or crayons	3–5 dried beans	10 or more plastic cups	10 or more index cards

LET'S TINKER!

In the fairy tale, Jack climbed up into the clouds and found a castle. **Make** your own cloud out of your materials. Which are soft and fluffy? What is hidden in your cloud? **Use** your materials to hide some treasure!

LET'S MAKE: MAGIC BEANS!

1. **Fold** a wet paper towel and place it inside a sandwich bag.

2. **Place** a few dried beans inside. You can **use** any beans, like black beans, pinto beans, or kidney beans. **Make sure** the beans are on top of the paper towel, so you can see them.

3. Close the sandwich bag and place it by a window.

4. Watch your beans for a week. What happens inside the bag?

5. Plant your seeds in the dirt if you want to watch them keep growing.

LET'S ENGINEER!

The MotMots read the story "Jack and the Beanstalk." They don't have any magic beans or giant beanstalks, but they would like to climb above the clouds.

How can the MotMots reach the clouds?

Build your own model of a beanstalk. How can you stack your materials to build a taller and taller stalk? How can you combine the materials so the stalk is taller? Can you build as high as your waist, your shoulders, or even the clouds?

PROJECT 7: DONE!
Get your sticker!

A **biography** is a story about a person's life, written by someone else. With the help of an adult, read this biography aloud.

Zaha Hadid

Zaha Hadid was born in Baghdad, Iraq, on October 31, 1930. In school she studied math and science. Then she became an architect. An architect is a person who designs buildings, bridges, and other structures.

Her designs were unique. They didn't look like any other buildings. Some had curved walls and wavy roofs. Some others looked like things in nature—one building was shaped like stones in a river.

Many people said that her unique buildings couldn't be built. They thought it would be too hard. But Zaha believed in her ideas. She kept drawing and designing.

Many years later, Zaha built her first building—a fire station. Then she built another building, and another. Soon she had buildings all over the world! She won awards that women had never won before.

Zaha never stopped believing in her designs. She did what she loved, no matter what people said. Her buildings show her brave ideas and determination.

opera house

art gallery

fire station

bridge

apartment building

You can learn new information from text and from pictures. Write a ✔ next to how you learned each of these facts about Zaha and her buildings.

Zaha was born in Iraq.

☐ text

☐ pictures

She studied math and science.

☐ text

☐ pictures

Zaha designed a bridge shaped like waves.

☐ text

☐ pictures

She won awards that women had never won before.

☐ text

☐ pictures

Some people thought her designs couldn't be built.

☐ text

☐ pictures

Answer each question according to the biography on page 58.

Did Zaha Hadid write this biography?

☐ yes

☐ no

What is an architect?

_____

_____

Circle Zaha's first building.

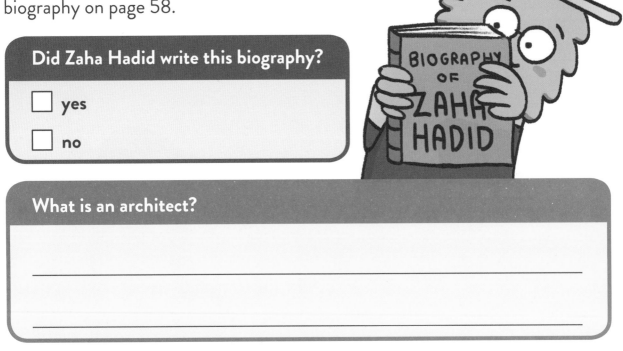

fire station

opera house

art gallery

What happened after many years that let Zaha know that believing in her ideas had worked?

☐ She studied math and science.

☐ She won awards that women had never won before.

☐ She designed a building with curved walls.

Circle a word that describes Zaha.

determined   bored   lazy

There are many words to describe Zaha's designs. Hunt around your home to find other objects that fit these descriptions. Then draw a picture of each one you find.

pointy

round

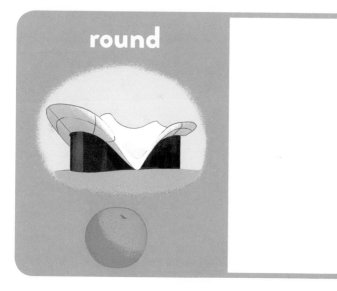

wavy

Zaha studied math and science in school so she could become an architect. Write about your favorite thing to study.

_____

_____

Zaha designed some buildings to look like things in nature, like stones, rivers, and sand. Look out your window or go outside. Draw one thing that you see in nature. Then label it.

_____

Draw a picture of your own building design that looks like what you saw outside.

Zaha kept designing buildings even when other people didn't believe in her designs or didn't want to build them. She was determined.

Write about and draw a time that you were determined. Describe something that you kept trying even when it wasn't easy.

LET'S START! GATHER THESE TOOLS AND MATERIALS.

Small cardboard box	Sandwich bag	6–8 bendable straws	6 or more craft sticks
Tape	Paper	Markers	Scissors (with an adult's help)	Cereal box

LET'S TINKER!

Look at the boxes and bags that your materials came in. What can you learn from the text? What about from the pictures? **Make** a new box or bag for one of your materials. **Draw** and write what you think should be on the package.

LET'S MAKE: BRIDGE CHALLENGE!

1. Cut a half-inch slit in the bottom of a bendable straw.

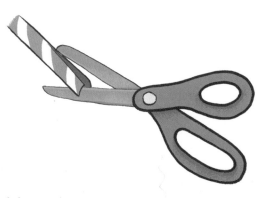

2. Get another bendable straw and stick the bottom of it into the slit of your first straw.

3. Repeat steps 1 and 2 with another 2 straws.

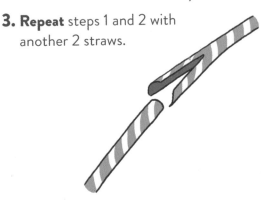

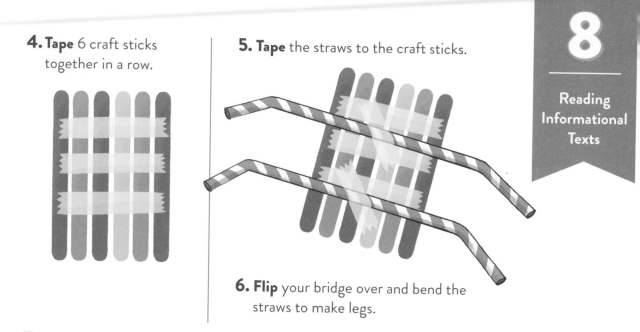

4. Tape 6 craft sticks together in a row.

5. Tape the straws to the craft sticks.

6. Flip your bridge over and bend the straws to make legs.

7. If your bridge is wobbly, **add** another set of straws to strengthen it. You can also **add** tape "feet" to secure the bridge to a surface, like a table.

8. Test your design like an architect. What can it hold on top? What would make it stronger?

LET'S ENGINEER!

Tinker Town needs a new fire station. The town is holding a competition for building designs. The building must be tall, strong, and large enough to fit three fire trucks. Each of the MotMots is planning a design.

How can each MotMot show his or her design to enter the competition?

Draw, build, make a model, or write about your own plan for a Tinker Town fire station. What shape will your design be? How tall can you make it? How will people know that it is a fire station? How can you share your ideas and design?

PROJECT 8: DONE!
Get your sticker!

Comparing Texts

A **fantasy story** is a fictional text that often includes wizards, monsters, magic, and other supernatural people, places, and things.

With the help of an adult, read each fantasy story aloud.

My First Flying Lesson

My dad gave me my first flying lesson today. He said, "Wing, think about the air rushing past you." I did. He told me to close my eyes. I did. He told me to get a running start and then fly. I ran! But I didn't fly.

Then I saw my friend Racer zoom by. He made flying look easy. I didn't want to move my wings because I was sad. But I tried again anyway. I flapped my wings, but nothing happened. I flapped them faster, but still nothing happened. Tomorrow I will try again. Flying is hard!

Learning to Fly

Hi, my name is Racer!

A few hours ago, I learned to fly! My mom took me outside for a lesson. I couldn't wait to begin—I knew just what I wanted to do.

First, I took a deep breath.

Next, I looked right and left to make sure that the air was clear.

Then, I flapped my wings as fast as I could.

Last, I kicked my feet off the ground, and I flew!

Flying is easy! It's fast and it's fun. Tomorrow I will try flying backward. Maybe I can fly upside down!

Draw a line to connect each quote from the story to the character who said it.

Flying is easy!

I flapped my wings, but nothing happened.

Tomorrow I will try flying backward.

I kicked my feet off the ground, and I flew!

Flying is hard!

Maybe I can fly upside down!

My dad gave me my first flying lesson today.

Compare the two characters from the stories, Wing and Racer.

WING

Write about and draw what happened during Wing's flying lesson.

Write about and draw what Wing thinks about flying.

Write about and draw what Wing will do tomorrow.

Write about and draw one way that Wing and Racer are the same.

What steps did Wing take to try to fly? Act it out!

RACER

Write about and draw what happened during Racer's flying lesson.

Write about and draw what Racer thinks about flying.

Write about and draw what Racer will do tomorrow.

Write about and draw one way that Wing and Racer are different.

What steps did Racer take to try to fly? Act it out!

Some texts tell stories, while other texts give information.

Read the diagram to learn information about dragonflies.

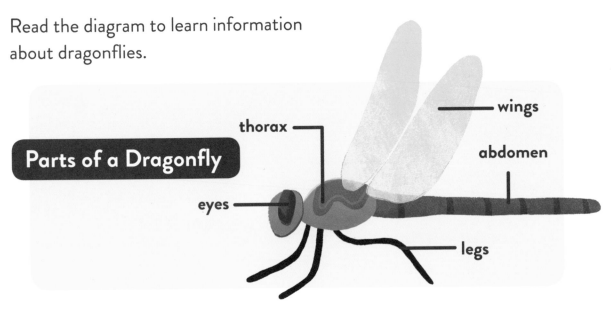

Parts of a Dragonfly

thorax

wings

abdomen

eyes

legs

Write something you learned about dragonflies.

_____

_____

_____

Write about and draw one thing you'd still like to learn about dragonflies.

_____

_____

_____

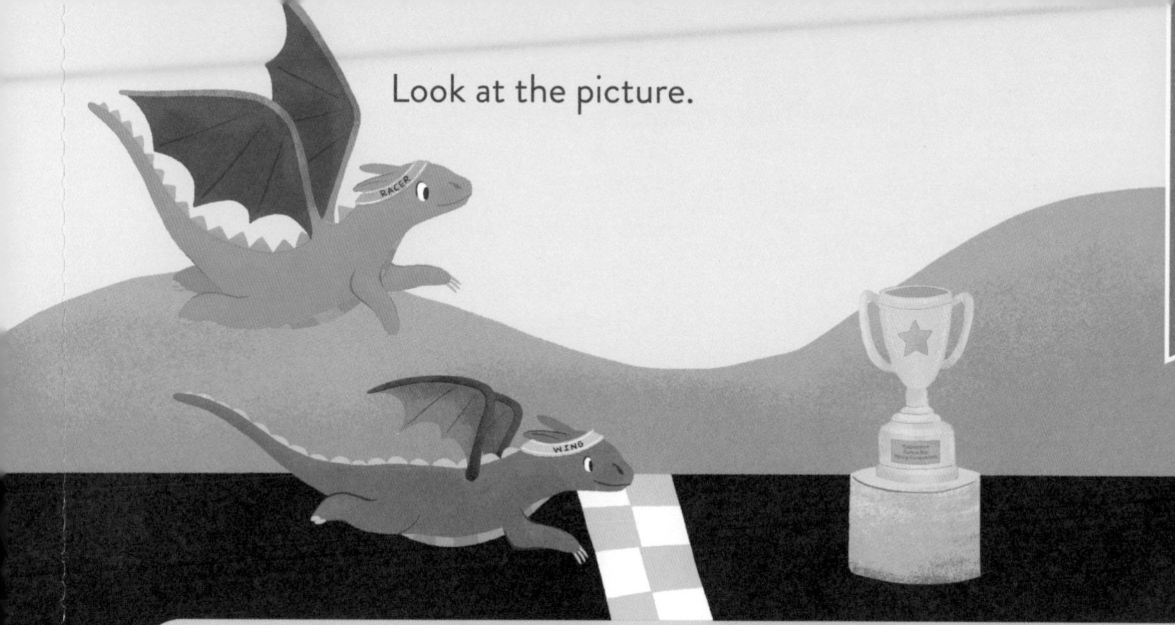

Write and draw your own story about the dragons above.

_____

_____

_____

LET'S START!

Paper

Scissors
(with an adult's help)

4–6 drinking straws

Markers

Tape

4–6 rubber bands

4–6 cotton balls

Craft sticks

Clothespins

LET'S TINKER!

Choose one of your materials. First, **say** one piece of information about it. Then **tell** one story about it! **Tell** a second story. How were they the same? How were they different?

LET'S MAKE: FLYING DRAGONFLY!

1. Cut a small square piece of paper, about the size of the palm of your hand.

2. Roll the paper around the end of a straw and tape it.

3. Fold over the end of the paper and tape it down.

4. Use a sticker from page 129 to add a dragonfly, another insect, or a fantasy animal.

5. Blow on the straw to watch your animal fly!

LET'S ENGINEER!

The MotMots are entering the Tinker Town Flying Cotton Ball Competition. Each MotMot designs a launcher. Then a cotton ball is pulled back and released to see who is the winner!

How can Frank send his cotton ball the farthest?

Send your own cotton balls flying with a rubber band around your pointer finger. How can you create a design to send your cotton ball farther? Does it matter if your finger is straight or bent? Do any rubber bands work better than others? What materials could work instead of a finger? **Compare** your designs.

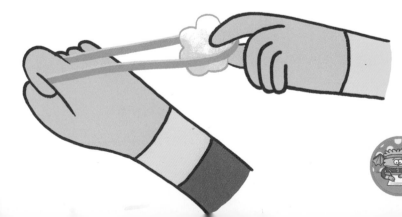

PROJECT 9: DONE!
Get your sticker!

Reading Comprehension

A **play** is a story acted out by actors, sometimes on a stage. The actors read their parts of the play from a **script**. With the help of an adult, read the script aloud.

The Flying Turtle

TURTLE: I want to see the world! But my legs are short. And my home is stuck on my back. So, I can't walk very fast.

DUCK: Maybe we can help you.

(The duck talks to his friend. They pick up a stick.)

DUCK: My friend and I will take you up into the sky! You can see the world. But you must promise not to say one word while we are flying.

TURTLE: Yes! I promise! Let's go!

DUCK: Okay. Bite this stick. Hold tight. And do not say one word!

(The ducks each take one end of the stick. The turtle bites the middle. They fly up in the sky. After a while, they pass a man below on the ground.)

MAN: What a sight! I have never seen a turtle fly!

TURTLE: Hello there!

(As soon as the turtle opens his mouth, he begins to fall . . .)

Write a line that each character may have said after the
turtle fell, and read it aloud.

Write about and draw how you think the play ends.

Read each of the turtle's lines below aloud. Look at his face to read the line with the correct expression.

"I want to see the world! But my legs are short. And my home is stuck on my back."

"Yes! I promise! Let's go!"

Read the duck's lines below aloud. Then draw a picture of what you think he may have looked like when he said each one.

"My friend and I will take you up into the sky!"

"Bite this stick. Hold tight."

Read the play on page 74 aloud by yourself or with a partner. Try using different voices for the characters.

Draw a line through the maze to all the places the turtle may have seen on his flight with the ducks.

Circle what the turtle wanted.

to have a stick　　　**to see the world**　　　**to make friends**

Why couldn't the turtle see the world? _____

_____

Circle the character who said, "You must promise not to say one word while we are flying."

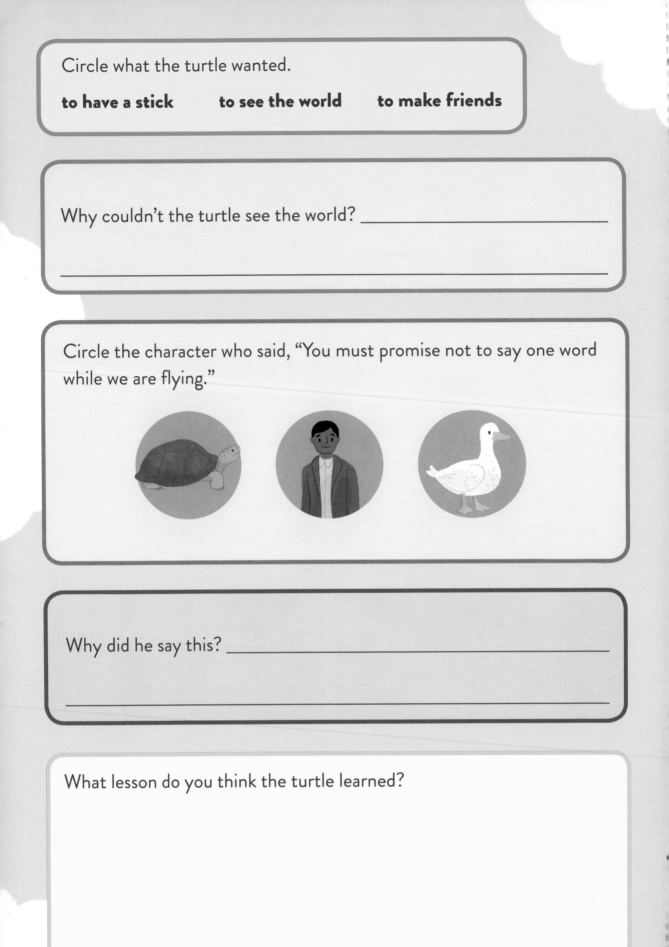

Why did he say this? _____

_____

What lesson do you think the turtle learned?

Write and draw to retell the play *The Flying Turtle*. What happened first, next, and last?

First, _____

_____

_____

_____

Next, _____

_____

_____

Last, _____

_____

_____

Use your fingers to retell the story, too! Point to your pinkie finger and tell what happens first. Use your other fingers to tell the next events. Then use your thumb to tell what happens last.

LET'S START! GATHER THESE TOOLS AND MATERIALS.

6 or more small round stones	Glue	Paint	Paintbrush
Markers	A few small paper bags	3–5 craft sticks	3–5 cotton balls

LET'S TINKER!

Imagine that your materials have voices. What would each sound like? What might they say? Can you make up a different voice for each material?

Life is Hard!

LET'S MAKE: TURTLE TOY!

1. **Find** 6 smooth round stones—1 large stone and 5 small stones.

2. **Arrange** your stones like a turtle: Lay your largest stone down—it will be a turtle shell. **Push** 5 stones under it to be 4 legs and a head.

3. Lift the shell stone and add a large drop of glue to the top of the 5 smaller stones. Then **press** the shell stone down on top.

4. Leave the turtle to dry for several hours.

5. Paint your turtle.

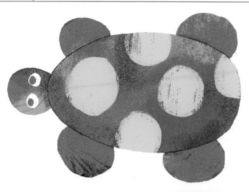

6. Act out your own turtle story! What does your turtle want? What stands in his or her way? How does he or she overcome that obstacle?

LET'S ENGINEER!

Brian and Enid are putting on a play about a turtle who wants to make new friends. He meets a lot of new animals along the way!

How can they make characters to tell their story?

Make characters for your own story with the materials. You can **add** stickers from page 129. Will you make animals, people, or something else— like robots or talking caterpillars? What story can you act out with your characters?

PROJECT 10: DONE!
Get your sticker!

Punctuation

Read the class trip form below. Trace the punctuation at the end of each sentence.

TINKER TOWN SCHOOL

We are taking a class trip to the Statue of Liberty!

The trip will be on April 4th.

The teachers on the trip will be
Mr. Game and Mrs. Play.

WEAR COMFORTABLE SHOES.
We will climb 354 steps to the top of the statue!

WHO IS GOING ON THE TRIP?

My full name is _Greg Thinker_ .

My birth date is _March 15, 2013_ .

My teacher's name is _Mrs. Play_ .

My three favorite trip snacks are _apples, crackers,_

and nuts .

**Bring your binoculars.
The Statue of Liberty's torch
is over 305 feet high!**

Every sentence has a punctuation mark at the end, like the following.

● A **period** is used at the end of a statement. A statement tells you something.

❓ A **question mark** is used to ask a question.

❗ An **exclamation point** is used to share a big feeling, like excitement.

Read each sentence. Then write the correct punctuation mark at the end.

 This is my first trip to New York City___

 How long will it take to get there___

 The Statue of Liberty is near Ellis Island___

 This is the best trip I've ever taken___

 Is the Statue of Liberty taller than my home___

 I am so excited to climb to the top___

The names of days and months should be capitalized. Write each date with a capital letter.

The trip is in _____.

april

It is on a _____.

saturday

The Statue of Liberty holds a tablet that

says _____.

july 4, 1776

The names of specific people should be capitalized. Write each name with a capital letter at the beginning of each word.

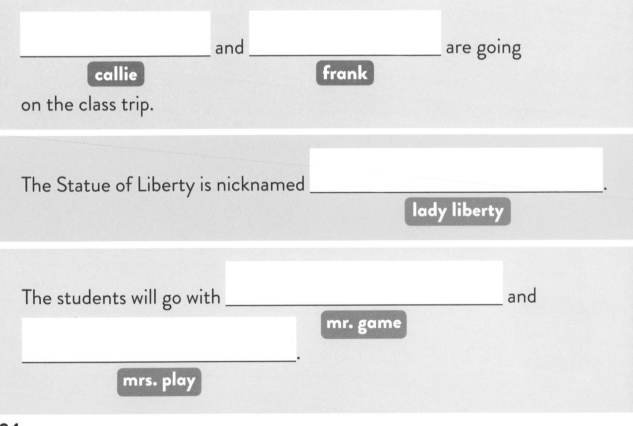

_____ and _____ are going

callie   frank

on the class trip.

The Statue of Liberty is nicknamed _____.

lady liberty

The students will go with _____ and

mr. game

_____.

mrs. play

A **comma** is used to separate groups of three or more items in a sentence.

Amelia is taking a notebook, a pen, and a pencil on the class trip.

Complete each sentence with the missing words and necessary commas. Include "and" before the last item.

Callie is taking _____

_____.

a pear   **a strawberry**   **a banana**

Enid is taking _____

_____.

a helicopter   **a truck**   **a boat**

Frank is taking _____

_____.

a hamburger   **a pickle**   **a hot dog**

Finish this sentence.

I would take _____.

A **possessive noun** uses an apostrophe (') to show that something belongs to another person or thing.

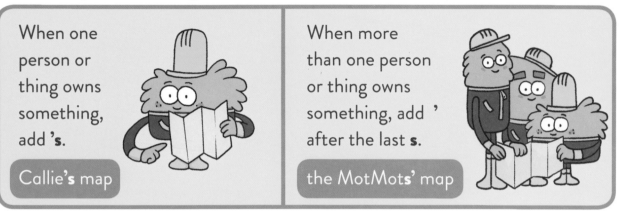

When one person or thing owns something, add **'s**.

Callie**'s** map

When more than one person or thing owns something, add **'** after the last **s**.

the MotMot**s'** map

The MotMots have many plans for their trip to New York City. Use an apostrophe to write each possessive noun correctly.

Amelia_____ plan is to draw in her notebook.

Dimitri_____ plan is to take pictures.

Brian_____ plan is to write a postcard.

The teachers_____ plan is busy!

Write a sentence about Enid's plan.

_____

_____

_____

Fill out the form. Use capital letters and punctuation where necessary.

CLASS TRIP!

My full name is _____.

My birth date is _____.

My teacher's name is _____.

My three favorite snacks are _____

_____.

Write about and draw where you want to go on a class trip.

_____

_____

_____

LET'S START! GATHER THESE TOOLS AND MATERIALS.

2–3 paper plates	Scissors (with an adult's help)	Glue	Crayons	Paper
20 or more dried beans	Egg carton		7 paper or plastic cups	Tape

LET'S TINKER!

Use your materials to make the shape of the following punctuation marks:

a period **.**   a question mark **?**   an exclamation point **!**

LET'S MAKE: LIBERTY CROWN!

1. Cut around the inside circle of a paper plate.

2. Cut off the bottom of the outer circle to make a crown.

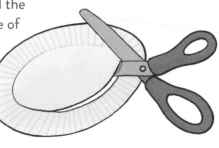

3. Draw lines to divide the leftover circle into 8 pieces and cut them out.

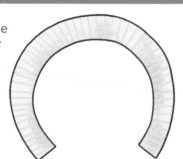

4. Glue 7 of the triangles to the crown, to match the statue's seven rays.

5. Color the crown with crayons.

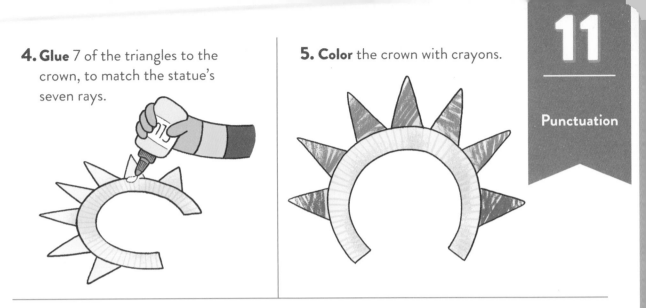

6. Some people think the Statue of Liberty's crown looks like the sun. **Write** a sentence about what you think the crown looks like. Which punctuation mark did you use at the end?

_____

_____

LET'S ENGINEER!

Callie has been saving money for a vacation at Topsy-Turvy Tinker Park. Each ride costs 1 token. She can buy 20 tokens and wants to go on a ride every day for a week.

How can Callie make sure that her tokens last all 7 days?

Use your beans as tokens. How can you sort the beans so there are some for each day? **Try** making a container for each day of the week. **Write** the name of each day of the week on the containers. **Remember** to capitalize them! Does Callie have enough for at least 1 ride per day? How many ways can you sort the beans?

PROJECT 11: DONE!
Get your sticker!

With the help of an adult, read the essay aloud.

Dinosaur Fossils

Dinosaurs lived on Earth before people lived on Earth. They are now extinct. That means that there are no dinosaurs alive today.

So how do we know so much about dinosaurs if we never lived with them? We learn about them from the fossils they left behind! People who study fossils are called paleontologists. They find fossils of dinosaur bones, eggs, teeth, and footprints all over the world!

Paleontologists dig for fossils in the ground. They use tools like shovels, axes, and brushes to uncover them. Then they wrap the fossils in plaster. This is so the fossils can be safely moved to labs to be studied. Paleontologists try to figure out what kind of dinosaur each fossil belonged to.

Fossils show that dinosaurs came in all different sizes. Some giants, like Titanosaurus, may have been 130 feet long when they were alive. That's longer than a basketball court! But some other dinosaur fossils are very small. The Microraptor was only a few feet long. It weighed about the same as a chicken.

Dinosaurs were amazing animals. We learn more all the time from studying their fossils. Who knows what we will find out next!

Find an example of each of these types of punctuation in the essay on page 90:

● Draw a ◯ around a period.

❓ Draw a ☐ around a question mark.

❗ Draw a △ around an exclamation mark.

Write the correct punctuation mark at the end of each sentence below.

Are there any fossils under my school____

I am so excited to learn about dinosaurs____

Callie-saurus would be a good dinosaur name____

Write one question you have about dinosaurs. Use a capital letter at the beginning of your sentence and a question mark at the end.

_____

_____

Use your finger to draw each type of end punctuation in the air.

Sentences can talk about the past, present, or future.

Write the correct form of each verb in the paleontologists' schedule.

YESTERDAY

I dug.

We _____.

He _____.

They brushed.

I scraped.

We _____.

I _____.

We look.

I drink.

They _____.

I hike.

We _____.

TOMORROW

I will eat.

We _____.

She will study.

We _____.

He _____.

They will wrap.

Write a sentence about each dinosaur and what is happening in each picture. Use a capital letter for the first word of each sentence and a punctuation mark at the end.

Velociraptor

_____

_____

_____

Baryonyx

_____

_____

_____

Titanosaurus

_____

_____

_____

Answer each question with a sentence. Use an "!" at the end of sentences that you are excited about.

What is your favorite animal?

_____

_____

Why is this animal the best?

_____

_____

What is one thing you'd like to learn about this animal?

_____

_____

Draw a picture of yourself with your favorite animal.

LET'S START!

1 cup flour	1 cup dirt	½ cup sand (or use more dirt)	1 cup water	Spoon	Small plastic toys or real objects that can get wet, like: a shell, an acorn, or a rock
Bowl	Tray	Paper	Pencil	8 or more craft sticks	Glue

LET'S TINKER!

Pick up one of your materials. **Play** with it and describe aloud what you are doing. For example, "I dig in the sand."

Then **say** the sentence again in the past tense, to describe how you would have used it yesterday. For example, "Yesterday I dug in the sand."

Can you say how you would play with each material today and yesterday? What about tomorrow?

LET'S MAKE: TOY FOSSIL DIG!

1. Mix the flour, dirt, sand, and 1 cup of water in a bowl.

2. Stir it until it's like thick mud. (If it's runny, add more dirt, sand, and flour.)

3. **Grab** a handful of the mud mixture and make a ball around a small toy (or something from outside, like a shell or rock). It will **feel** like making a snowball around your "fossil"! **Try** making several balls, each with a different item inside.

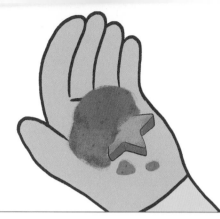

4. **Lay** the mud balls on a tray to dry, either inside or outside in the sun. After a few hours, **flip** them over so that both sides dry.

5. After they have dried overnight, **dig** for your very own fossils using the craft sticks!

LET'S ENGINEER!

Callie took a trip to the dinosaur museum. She saw fossils of bones, footprints, and even dinosaur poop!

How can she share the facts she learned about dinosaurs with her friends?

Make your own dinosaur exhibit with models of fossils. You can **make** eggs, teeth, or even a whole dinosaur. Then **write** labels for your exhibit. You can **share** names and facts, or even ask questions you still have about dinosaurs!

PROJECT 12: DONE!
Get your sticker!

Telling a Story

A **timeline** can be used to share information about an event or a story. It shows the order that things happened from the past to the present. With the help of an adult, read the timeline aloud. Then answer each question.

The First Moon Landing

The Apollo 11 spacecraft launched from Earth into space. Inside were Neil Armstrong, Buzz Aldrin, and Michael Collins.

July 16, 1969

Four days later, Armstrong and Aldrin landed a part of their spacecraft on the moon.

July 20, 1969

Write a ✔ next to the event that happened first.

☐ The Apollo 11 spacecraft launched from Earth.

☐ Armstrong and Aldrin landed a part of their spacecraft on the moon.

Write a ✔ next to the event that happened last.

☐ The astronauts collected moon soil.

☐ The astronauts returned to Earth.

Armstrong opened the hatch, climbed down nine steps, and became the first person to walk on the moon!

Twenty minutes later, Aldrin joined him on the moon. They collected some moon soil to bring back home.

The three astronauts returned safely to Earth. Since then, twenty-one more people have traveled to the moon.

July 21, 1969

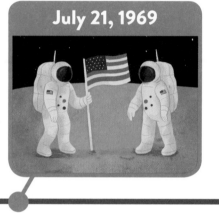

July 21, 1969

July 24, 1969

On what date did the Apollo 11 spacecraft launch into space?

_____

Who took the first steps on the moon?

_____

How many astronauts walked on the moon on July 21, 1969?

_____

What did the astronauts bring back from the moon?

_____

The timeline on pages 98 and 99 tells about an event: the first moon landing. Stories can also tell about events. They can be about your life—events that were happy, important, silly, or more. Everyone has stories to tell!

Write about and draw the first thing you did today.

Where were you?

Write about and draw a time you ate a food that surprised you.

What did you say?

Write about and draw a time you went somewhere new.

How did you feel?

Write about and draw a time you and your family laughed.

What did it sound like?

The timeline on pages 98 and 99 tells about what happened first, next, and last when Neil Armstrong walked on the moon.

Write and draw your own timeline that tells about an event from your life. Use your writing on pages 100 and 101 for ideas.

Title: _____

First, I _____

_____.

PAST

Next, I _____

_____.

Circle the animal that is almost completely transparent.

Draw a picture of the animal with tentacles.

Circle the part of the anglerfish that glows.

Draw lines to match each animal with the reason why it uses bioluminescence.

to attract prey to eat

to scare predators away

to hide from predators

Many other kinds of animals use their special parts to help them survive. Read about each animal and answer the questions.

WOODPECKERS have sticky tongues.

CHAMELEONS have very fast tongues.

GIRAFFES have long tongues.

Which of these animals do you think reaches far away for food?

_____

Why? _____

_____

Which of these animals do you think catches food that's moving quickly?

_____

Why? _____

_____

PORCUPINES
have sharp quills.

TURTLES
have heavy and hard shells.

ARMADILLOS
have tough plates of armor.

Which of these animals do you think is too slow to run from danger?

_____

Why? _____

_____

Which of these animals do you think can poke a predator?

_____

Why? _____

_____

Hunt around the inside and outside of your home. Write about and draw the animals that you see.

Circle any special body parts that help these animals survive.

Write facts about your favorite animal that you saw.

Animal's name: _____

Does it live inside or outside? _____

How does it move? _____

_____

Does it live alone or with other animals? _____

_____

Why is it your favorite animal that you saw? _____

_____

Write and draw other facts you know about this animal.

Is it fast or slow? How does it protect itself? Can it fly? How many legs does it have? What does it eat?

LET'S START! GATHER THESE TOOLS AND MATERIALS.

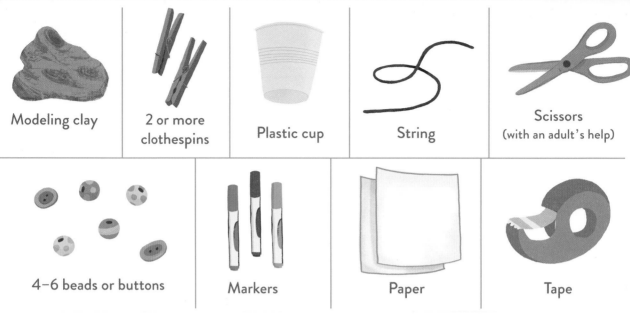

Modeling clay	2 or more clothespins	Plastic cup	String	Scissors (with an adult's help)
4–6 beads or buttons	Markers	Paper	Tape	

LET'S TINKER!

Make a model of your favorite animal with the materials. What shape is it? How big or small is it? Does it swim or fly? What body parts can you make?

LET'S MAKE: ANGLERFISH GAME!

1. With the help of an adult, **use** scissors to poke a small hole in the center of the bottom of a plastic cup.

2. Cut a 12-inch piece of string. **Thread** one end of the string through the bottom of the cup. **Use** a piece of tape in the bottom of the cup to stick it in place.

3. Tie a bead (or button) to the other end of the string. If the bead is very small, **tie** on a few more.

4. Use paper and a marker to add eyes and teeth to your cup so it looks like a fish.

5. Hold the cup in your hand. **Flip** the bead in the air and catch it in the cup, just like an anglerfish catching prey in its jaws.

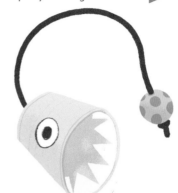

LET'S ENGINEER!

The MotMots are on an animal safari in the park. They love the sandwiches that Dimitri packed for their picnic lunch. They want to be able to make the sandwiches themselves!

How can Dimitri share the recipe for his special sandwiches?

Write and draw your own instructions about how to make your favorite sandwich or snack. What ingredients and tools do you need? What do you do first? Next? And last? **Try** reading your instructions to a family member. **Ask** him or her to make your recipe using your instructions to see if they work!

PROJECT 14: DONE!
Get your sticker!

A **cinquain poem** has five lines that follow a special pattern. Read the cinquain poem aloud.

At Night
by Cora

Bedtime
Dark, quiet
Reading, resting, thinking
Happy in my bed
Sleep

A **free verse poem** has no patterns or rules. Read the free verse poem aloud.

Dark Night
by Eli

So black.
I can't see anything.
It's time to go to bed.
BUT.
I'm scared!
Too much fear to fall asleep.
I wish I had a light.
A bright spot for the dark night.

Write and draw research questions about the poems.

? What is one thing you wonder about Cora's bedtime?

? What is one thing you wonder about Eli's bedtime?

What question do you have for Cora about feeling happy?

What question do you have for Eli about feeling scared?

Write what you think Cora and Eli would say if you asked them these questions.

Poems express thoughts and feelings. Write sentences and draw some of your thoughts and feelings.

My name: _____

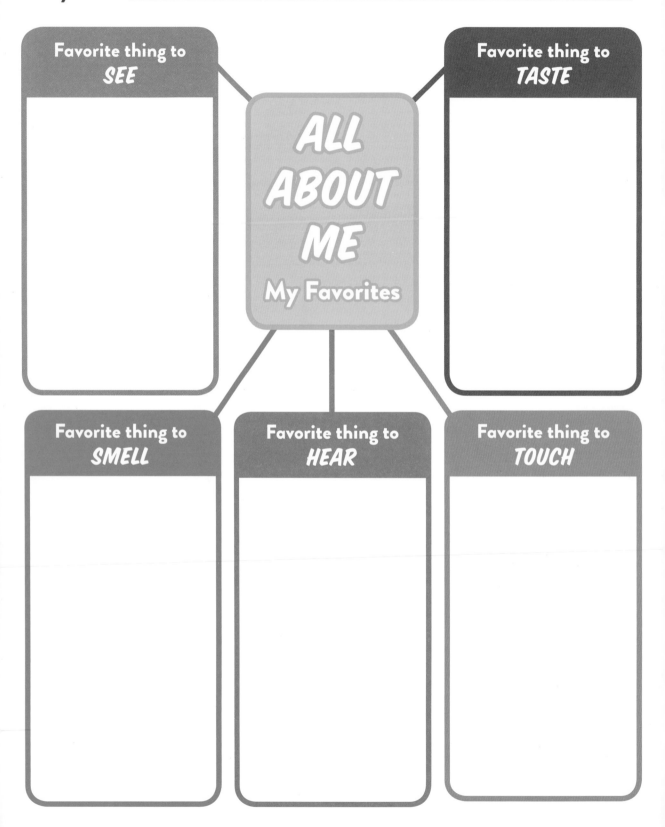

Favorite thing to
SEE

Favorite thing to
TASTE

ALL
ABOUT
ME
My Favorites

Favorite thing to
SMELL

Favorite thing to
HEAR

Favorite thing to
TOUCH

Write about and draw something that makes you feel:

excited	nervous

brave	cheerful

curious	silly

A cinquain poem always has five lines that follow a special pattern.

My Pet ← title

Cat ← topic

Soft, fluffy ← adjectives that describe the topic

Petting, purring, playing ← verbs, action words

Nervous he'll scratch me ← a phrase about feelings

Friend ← describes the topic

Write your own cinquain poem about one of your favorite things. Look at your research on pages 116 and 117 for ideas of what to write about.

_____

_____, _____

_____, _____, _____

_____

_____

Use the research you've gathered from pages 116 and 117 to write your own free verse poem. Write about your favorites, memories, or even write made-up stories.

_____

_____

_____

_____

_____

_____

_____

_____

_____

_____

_____

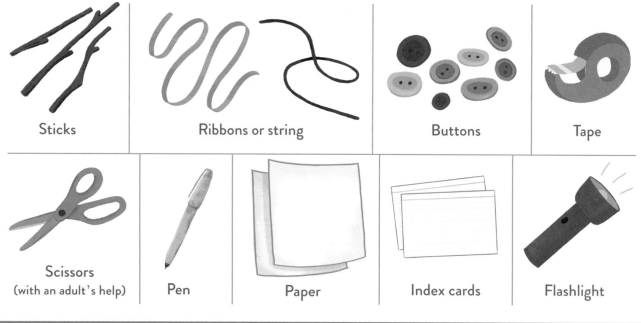

Sticks	Ribbons or string	Buttons	Tape
Scissors (with an adult's help)	Pen	Paper	Index cards	Flashlight

LET'S TINKER!

Research how light and dark affect these materials. **Turn** a light on and off. How do they look? **Go** outside. Do they look different in the sun? **Try** the flashlight, too. Which can you see the best in the dark?

LET'S MAKE: STORY STICK!

1. Decorate your stick with your choice of ribbons, string, buttons, and tape.

2. Find one partner (or more!) to start the game.

3. Hold the story stick. **Say** one sentence to start a story. For example, "The monster walked to the park."

4. Pass the stick to the next person. Now they **continue** the story by saying one sentence about what happens next. For example, "When the monster got to the park, he went on a swing!"

5. Pass the stick until everyone has had one turn. Then it's your turn again. **Keep passing** the stick and taking turns until the story is done.

LET'S ENGINEER!

Callie is afraid of the dark. She wants to know if her friends are, too, so they can help each other feel better.

How can she find out how her friends feel about the dark?

Ask your friends and family members questions about the dark. What questions will you ask to learn how they feel? Then **make** something to help someone who is afraid of the dark. **Try** making a night-light, a poem, or even a dream catcher. Which do you think would help? **Ask** questions to find out!

PROJECT 15: DONE!
Get your sticker!

ANSWER KEY

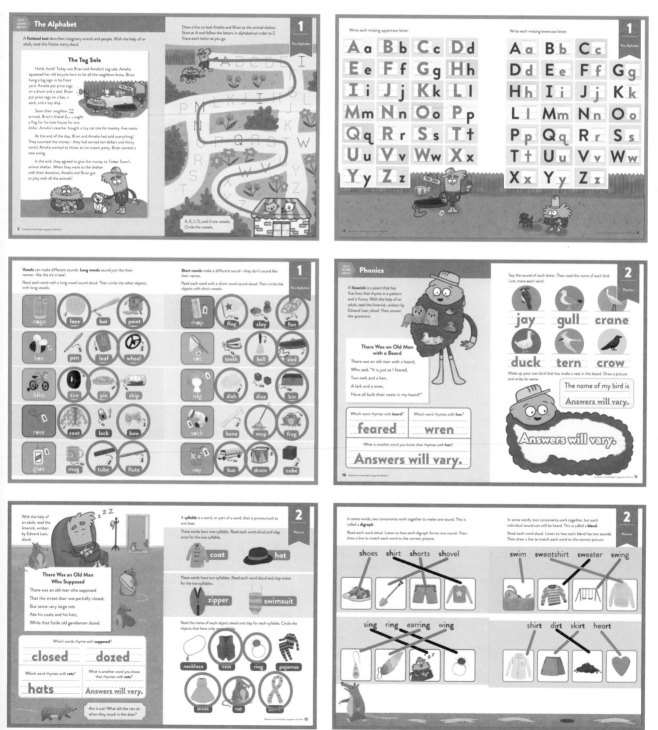

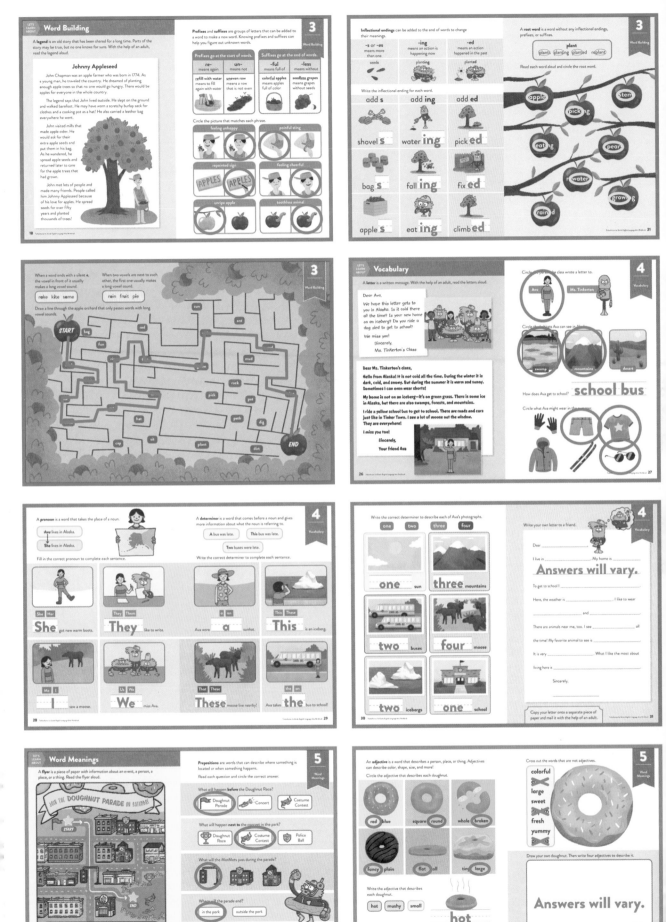

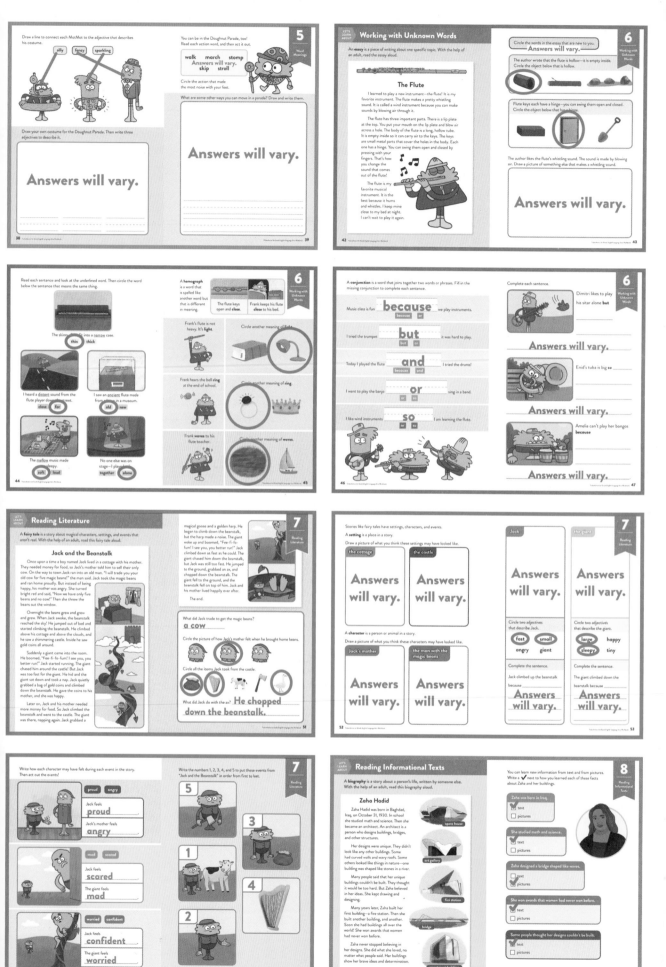

Page 5 — Word Meanings

Draw a line to connect each MotMot to the adjective that describes his costume.

silly   fancy   sparkling

Draw your own costume for the Doughnut Parade. Then write three adjectives to describe it.

Answers will vary.

You can be in the Doughnut Parade, too! Read each action word, and then act it out.

walk   march   stomp
Answers will vary.
skip   stroll

Circle the action that made the most noise with your feet.

What are some other ways you can move in a parade? Draw and write them.

Answers will vary.

Page 6 — Working with Unknown Words

An **essay** is a piece of writing about one specific topic. With the help of an adult, read the essay aloud.

The Flute

I learned to play a new instrument—the flute! It is my favorite instrument. The flute makes a pretty whistling sound. It is called a wind instrument because you can make sounds by blowing air through it.

The flute has three important parts. There is a lip plate at the top. You put your mouth on the lip plate and blow air across a hole. The body of the flute is a long, hollow tube. It is empty inside so it can carry air to the keys. The keys are small metal parts that cover the holes in the body. Each one has a hinge. You can swing them open and closed by pressing with your fingers. That's how you change the sound that comes out of the flute!

The flute is my favorite musical instrument. It is the best because it hums and whistles. I keep mine close to my bed at night. I can't wait to play it again.

Circle the words in the essay that are new to you.
Answers will vary.

The author wrote that the flute is hollow—it is empty inside. Circle the object below that is hollow.

Flute keys each have a hinge—you can swing them open and closed. Circle the object below that has a hinge.

The author likes the flute's whistling sound. The sound is made by blowing air. Draw a picture of something else that makes a whistling sound.

Answers will vary.

Page 6 (cont.) — Working with Unknown Words

Read each sentence and look at the underlined word. Then circle the word below the sentence that means the same thing.

The skinny flute fit into a narrow case. — thin / thick

I heard a distant sound from the flute player down the street. — close / far

I saw an ancient flute made from stone in a museum. — old / new

The mellow music made me sleepy. — soft / loud

No one else was on stage—I played alone. — together / alone

A **homograph** is a word that is spelled like another word but that is different in meaning.

The flute keys open and close.
Frank keeps his flute close to his bed.

Frank's flute is not heavy. It's light. — Circle another meaning of light.

Frank hears the bell ring at the end of school. — Circle another meaning of ring.

Frank waves to his flute teacher. — Circle another meaning of waves.

Page 6 (cont.) — Conjunctions

A **conjunction** is a word that joins together two words or phrases. Fill in the missing conjunction to complete each sentence.

Music class is fun **because** we play instruments. (because / or)

I tried the trumpet **but** it was hard to play. (but / or)

Today I played the flute **and** I tried the drums! (because / and)

I went to play the banjo **or** sing in a band. (or / but)

I like wind instruments **so** I am learning the flute. (or / so)

Complete each sentence.

Dimitri likes to play his sitar alone but **Answers will vary.**

Enid's tuba is big so **Answers will vary.**

Amelia can't play her bongos because **Answers will vary.**

Page 7 — Reading Literature

A **fairy tale** is a story about magical characters, settings, and events that aren't real. With the help of an adult, read this fairy tale aloud.

Jack and the Beanstalk

Once upon a time a boy named Jack lived in a cottage with his mother. They needed money for food, so Jack's mother told him to sell their only cow. On the way to town Jack ran into an old man. "I will trade your old cow for five magic beans!" the man said. Jack took the magic beans and ran home proudly. But instead of being happy, his mother was angry. She turned bright red and said, "Now we have only five beans and no cow!" Then she threw the beans out the window.

Overnight the beans grew and grew. When Jack awoke, the beanstalk reached the sky! He jumped out of bed and started climbing the beanstalk. He climbed above his cottage and above the clouds, and he saw a shimmering castle. Inside he saw gold coins all around.

Suddenly a giant came into the room. He boomed, "Fee-fi-fo-fum!" Jack started running. The giant chased him around the castle! But Jack was too fast for the giant. He hid and the giant sat down and took a nap. Jack quietly grabbed a bag of gold coins and climbed down the beanstalk. He gave the coins to his mother, and she was happy.

Later on, Jack and his mother needed more money for food. So Jack climbed the beanstalk and went to the castle. The giant was there, napping again. Jack grabbed a magical goose and a golden harp. He began to climb down the beanstalk, but the harp made a noise. The giant woke up and boomed, "Fee-fi-fo-fum! I see you, you better run!" Jack climbed down as fast as he could. The giant chased him down the beanstalk, but Jack was still too fast. He jumped to the ground, grabbed an ax, and chopped down the beanstalk. The giant fell to the ground, and the beanstalk fell on top of him. Jack and his mother lived happily ever after.

The end.

What did Jack trade to get the magic beans?
a cow

Circle the picture of how Jack's mother felt when she brought home beans.

Circle all the items Jack took from the castle.

What did Jack do with the ax? **He chopped down the beanstalk.**

Page 7 (cont.)

Stories like fairy tales have settings, characters, and events.

A **setting** is a place in a story. Draw a picture of what you think these settings may have looked like.

the cottage — **Answers will vary.**
the castle — **Answers will vary.**

A **character** is a person or animal in a story. Draw a picture of what you think these characters may have looked like.

Jack's mother — **Answers will vary.**
the man with the magic beans — **Answers will vary.**

Jack — **Answers will vary.**
the giant — **Answers will vary.**

Circle two adjectives that describe Jack. — fast / small / angry / giant

Circle two adjectives that describe the giant. — large / sleepy / happy / tiny

Complete the sentence.
Jack climbed up the beanstalk because **Answers will vary.**

The giant climbed down the beanstalk because **Answers will vary.**

Page 7 (cont.)

Write how each character may have felt during each event in the story. Then act out the events!

Jack feels **proud** (proud / angry)
Jack's mother feels **angry**

Jack feels **scared** (mad / scared)
The giant feels **mad**

Jack feels **confident** (worried / confident)
The giant feels **worried**

Write the numbers 1, 2, 3, 4, and 5 to put these events from "Jack and the Beanstalk" in order from first to last.

5, 3, 1, 4, 2

Page 8 — Reading Informational Texts

A **biography** is a story about a person's life, written by someone else. With the help of an adult, read this biography aloud.

Zaha Hadid

Zaha Hadid was born in Baghdad, Iraq, on October 31, 1930. In school she studied math and science. Then she became an architect. An architect is a person who designs buildings, bridges, and other structures.

Her designs were unique. They didn't look like any other buildings. Some had curved walls and wavy roofs. Some others looked like things in nature—one building was shaped like stones in a river.

Many people said that her unique buildings couldn't be built. They thought it would be too hard. But Zaha believed in her ideas. She kept drawing and designing.

Many years later, Zaha built her first building—a fire station. Then she built another building, and another. Soon she had buildings all over the world! She won awards that women had never won before.

Zaha never stopped believing in her designs. She did what she loved, no matter what people said. Her buildings show her brave ideas and determination.

(labels: opera house, art gallery, fire station, bridge, apartment building)

You can learn new information from text and from pictures. Write a ✔ next to how you learned each of these facts about Zaha and her buildings.

Zaha was born in Iraq. — ✔ text / pictures

She studied math and science. — ✔ text / pictures

Zaha designed a bridge shaped like waves. — text / ✔ pictures

She won awards that women had never won before. — ✔ text / pictures

Some people thought her designs couldn't be built. — ✔ text / pictures

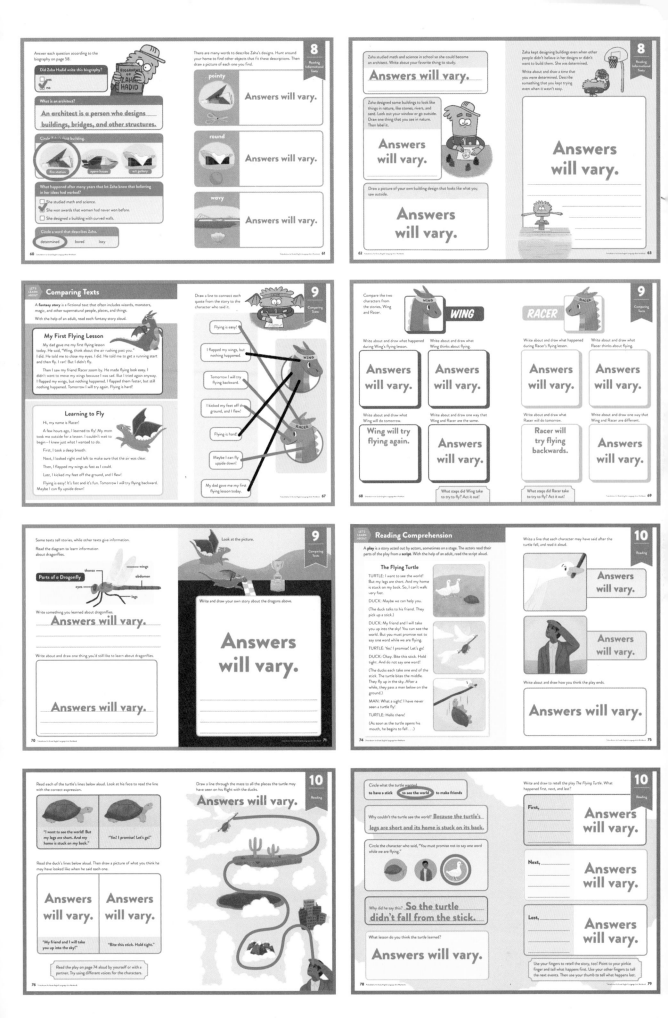

Pages 60–61 (Unit 8 — Reading Informational Texts)

Answer each question according to the biography on page 58.

Did Zaha Hadid write this biography?
- ☐ yes
- ☑ no

What is an architect?
An architect is a person who designs buildings, bridges, and other structures.

Circle Zaha's first building.
(fire station) ⟵ circled / space house / art gallery

What happened after many years that let Zaha know that believing in her ideas had worked?
- ☐ She studied math and science.
- ☑ She won awards that women had never won before.
- ☐ She designed a building with curved walls.

Circle a word that describes Zaha.
(determined) ⟵ circled   bored   lazy

There are many words to describe Zaha's designs. Hunt around your home to find other objects that fit these descriptions. Then draw a picture of each one you find.

pointy — Answers will vary.
round — Answers will vary.
wavy — Answers will vary.

Pages 62–63 (Unit 8 — Reading Informational Texts)

Zaha studied math and science in school so she could become an architect. Write about your favorite thing to study.
Answers will vary.

Zaha designed some buildings to look like things in nature, like stones, rivers, and sand. Look out your window or go outside. Draw one thing that you see in nature. Then label it.
Answers will vary.

Draw a picture of your own building design that looks like what you saw outside.
Answers will vary.

Zaha kept designing buildings even when other people didn't believe in her designs or didn't want to build them. She was determined.

Write about and draw a time that you were determined. Describe something that you kept trying even when it wasn't easy.
Answers will vary.

Pages 66–67 (Unit 9 — Comparing Texts)

Comparing Texts

A **fantasy story** is a fictional text that often includes wizards, monsters, magic, and other supernatural people, places, and things.

With the help of an adult, read each fantasy story aloud.

My First Flying Lesson

My dad gave me my first flying lesson today. He said, "Wing, think about the air rushing past you." I did. He told me to close my eyes. I did. He told me to get a running start and then fly. I ran! But I didn't fly.

Then I saw my friend Racer zoom by. He made flying look easy. I didn't want to move my wings because I was sad. But I tried again anyway. I flapped my wings, but nothing happened. I flapped them faster, but still nothing happened. Tomorrow I will try again. Flying is hard!

Learning to Fly

Hi, my name is Racer!

A few hours ago, I learned to fly! My mom took me outside for a lesson. I couldn't wait to begin—I knew just what I wanted to do.

First, I took a deep breath.

Next, I looked right and left to make sure that the air was clear.

Then, I flapped my wings as fast as I could.

Last, I kicked my feet off the ground, and I flew!

Flying is easy! It's fast and it's fun. Tomorrow I will try flying backward. Maybe I can fly upside down!

Draw a line to connect each quote from the story to the character who said it.

- Flying is easy!
- I flapped my wings, but nothing happened.
- Tomorrow I will try flying backward.
- I kicked my feet off the ground, and I flew!
- Flying is hard!
- Maybe I can fly upside down!
- My dad gave me my first flying lesson today.

WING
RACER

Pages 68–69 (Unit 9 — Comparing Texts)

Compare the two characters from the stories, Wing and Racer.

WING

Write about and draw what happened during Wing's flying lesson.
Answers will vary.

Write about and draw what Wing thinks about flying.
Answers will vary.

Write about and draw what Wing will do tomorrow.
Wing will try flying again.

Write about and draw one way that Wing and Racer are the same.
Answers will vary.

What steps did Wing take to try to fly? Act it out!

RACER

Write about and draw what happened during Racer's flying lesson.
Answers will vary.

Write about and draw what Racer thinks about flying.
Answers will vary.

Write about and draw what Racer will do tomorrow.
Racer will try flying backwards.

Write about and draw one way that Wing and Racer are different.
Answers will vary.

What steps did Racer take to try to fly? Act it out!

Pages 70–71 (Unit 9 — Comparing Texts)

Some texts tell stories, while other texts give information.

Read the diagram to learn information about dragonflies.

Parts of a Dragonfly
- thorax
- wings
- abdomen
- eyes
- legs

Write something you learned about dragonflies.
Answers will vary.

Write about and draw one thing you'd still like to learn about dragonflies.
Answers will vary.

Look at the picture.

Write and draw your own story about the dragons above.
Answers will vary.

Pages 74–75 (Unit 10 — Reading Comprehension)

Reading Comprehension

A **play** is a story acted out by actors, sometimes on a stage. The actors read their parts of the play from a **script**. With the help of an adult, read the script aloud.

The Flying Turtle

TURTLE: I want to see the world! But my legs are short. And my home is stuck on my back. So, I can't walk very fast.

DUCK: Maybe we can help you.

(The duck talks to his friend. They pick up a stick.)

DUCK: My friend and I will take you up into the sky! You can see the world. But you must promise not to say one word while we are flying.

TURTLE: Yes! I promise! Let's go!

DUCK: Okay. Bite this stick. Hold tight. And do not say one word!

(The ducks each take one end of the stick. The turtle bites the middle. They fly up into the sky. After a while, they pass a man below on the ground.)

MAN: What a sight! I have never seen a turtle fly!

TURTLE: Hello there!

(As soon as the turtle opens his mouth, he begins to fall . . .)

Write a line that each character may have said after the turtle fell, and read it aloud.
Answers will vary.
Answers will vary.

Write about and draw how you think the play ends.
Answers will vary.

Pages 76–77 (Unit 10 — Reading)

Read each of the turtle's lines below aloud. Look at his face to read the line with the correct expression.

"I want to see the world! But my legs are short. And my home is stuck on my back."

"Yes! I promise! Let's go!"

Read the duck's lines below aloud. Then draw a picture of what you think he may have looked like when he said each one.

Answers will vary. | Answers will vary.

"My friend and I will take you up into the sky!"

"Bite this stick. Hold tight."

Read the play on page 74 aloud by yourself or with a partner. Try using different voices for the characters.

Draw a line through the maze to all the places the turtle may have seen on his flight with the ducks.
Answers will vary.

Pages 78–79 (Unit 10 — Reading)

Circle what the turtle wanted.
to have a stick   (to see the world) ⟵ circled   to make friends

Why couldn't the turtle see the world? Because the turtle's legs are short and its home is stuck on its back.

Circle the character who said, "You must promise not to say one word while we are flying."
(duck is circled)

Why did he say this? So the turtle didn't fall from the stick.

What lesson do you think the turtle learned?
Answers will vary.

Write and draw to retell the play The Flying Turtle. What happened first, next, and last?

First, Answers will vary.
Next, Answers will vary.
Last, Answers will vary.

Use your fingers to retell the story, too! Point to your pinkie finger and tell what happens first. Use your other fingers to tell the next events. Then use your thumb to tell what happens last.

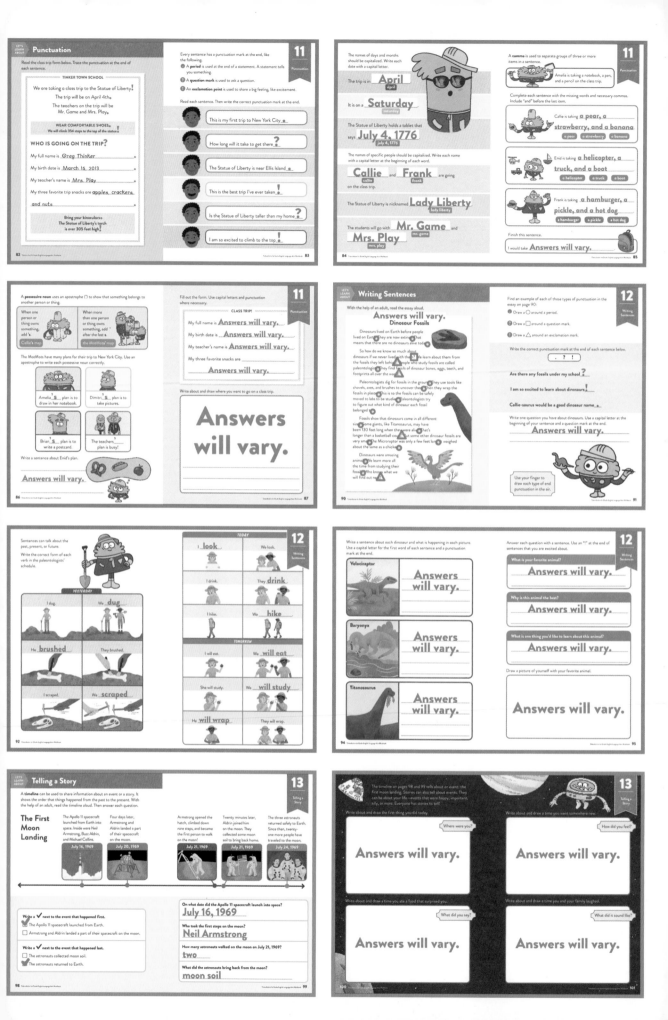

Punctuation

Read the class trip form below. Trace the punctuation at the end of each sentence.

TINKER TOWN SCHOOL

We are taking a class trip to the Statue of Liberty!
The trip will be on April 4th.
The teachers on the trip will be Mr. Game and Mrs. Play.

WEAR COMFORTABLE SHOES.
We will climb 354 steps to the top of the statue.

WHO IS GOING ON THE TRIP?

My full name is **Greg Thinker**.
My birth date is **March 15, 2013**.
My teacher's name is **Mrs. Play**.
My three favorite trip snacks are **apples, crackers, and nuts**.

Bring your binoculars.
The Statue of Liberty's torch is over 305 feet high!

Every sentence has a punctuation mark at the end, like the following.

1 A **period** is used at the end of a statement. A statement tells you something.
2 A **question mark** is used to ask a question.
3 An **exclamation point** is used to share a big feeling, like excitement.

Read each sentence. Then write the correct punctuation mark at the end.

- This is my first trip to New York City **.**
- How long will it take to get there **?**
- The Statue of Liberty is near Ellis Island **.**
- This is the best trip I've ever taken **!**
- Is the Statue of Liberty taller than my home **?**
- I am so excited to climb to the top **!**

The names of days and months should be capitalized. Write each date with a capital letter.

The trip is in **April**
It is on a **Saturday**
The Statue of Liberty holds a tablet that says **July 4, 1776**

The names of specific people should be capitalized. Write each name with a capital letter at the beginning of each word.

Callie and **Frank** are going on the class trip.

The Statue of Liberty is nicknamed **Lady Liberty**

The students will go with **Mr. Game** and **Mrs. Play**

A **comma** is used to separate groups of three or more items in a sentence.

Amelia is taking a notebook, a pen, and a pencil on the class trip.

Complete each sentence with the missing words and necessary commas. Include "and" before the last item.

Callie is taking **a pear, a strawberry, and a banana**

Enid is taking **a helicopter, a truck, and a boat**

Frank is taking **a hamburger, a pickle, and a hot dog**

Finish this sentence.

I would take **Answers will vary.**

A **possessive noun** uses an apostrophe (') to show that something belongs to another person or thing.

When one person or thing owns something, add 's.
When more than one person or thing owns something, add an ' after the last s.

The MotMots have many plans for their trip to New York City. Use an apostrophe to write each possessive noun correctly.

Amelia**'s** plan is to draw in her notebook.
Dimitri**'s** plan is to take pictures.
Brian**'s** plan is to write a postcard.
The teachers**'** plan is busy!

Write a sentence about Enid's plan.
Answers will vary.

Fill out the form. Use capital letters and punctuation where necessary.

CLASS TRIP!

My full name is **Answers will vary.**
My birth date is **Answers will vary.**
My teacher's name is **Answers will vary.**
My three favorite snacks are **Answers will vary.**

Write about and draw where you want to go on a class trip.

Answers will vary.

Writing Sentences

With the help of an adult, read the essay aloud.

Dinosaur Fossils

Answers will vary.

Find an example of each of these types of punctuation in the essay on page 90.
1 Draw a ○ around a period.
2 Draw a □ around a question mark.
3 Draw a △ around an exclamation mark.

Write the correct punctuation mark at the end of each sentence below.
. ? !

Are there any fossils under my school **?**
I am so excited to learn about dinosaurs **!**
Callie-saurus would be a good dinosaur name **.**

Write one question you have about dinosaurs. Use a capital letter at the beginning of your sentence and a question mark at the end.
Answers will vary.

Sentences can talk about the past, present, or future.

Write the correct form of each verb in the paleontologists' schedule.

YESTERDAY
I dug. We **dug**
He **brushed** They brushed.
I scraped. We **scraped**

TODAY
I **look** We look.
I drink. They **drink**
I hike. We **hike**

TOMORROW
I will eat. We **will eat**
She will study. We **will study**
He **will wrap** They will wrap.

Write a sentence about each dinosaur and what is happening in each picture. Use a capital letter for the first word of each sentence and a punctuation mark at the end.

Velociraptor — Answers will vary.
Baryonyx — Answers will vary.
Titanosaurus — Answers will vary.

Answer each question with a sentence. Use an "!" at the end of sentences that you are excited about.

What is your favorite animal? **Answers will vary.**
Why is this animal the best? **Answers will vary.**
What is one thing you'd like to learn about this animal? **Answers will vary.**

Draw a picture of yourself with your favorite animal.
Answers will vary.

Telling a Story

A **timeline** can be used to share information about an event or a story. It shows the order that things happened from the past to the present. With the help of an adult, read the timeline aloud. Then answer each question.

The First Moon Landing

The Apollo 11 spacecraft launched from Earth into space. Inside were Neil Armstrong, Buzz Aldrin, and Michael Collins.
July 16, 1969

Four days later, Armstrong and Aldrin landed a part of their spacecraft on the moon.
July 20, 1969

Armstrong opened the hatch, climbed down nine steps, and became the first person to walk on the moon!
July 21, 1969

Twenty minutes later, Aldrin joined him on the moon. They collected some moon soil to bring back home.
July 21, 1969

The three astronauts returned safely to Earth. Since then, twenty-one more people have traveled to the moon.
July 24, 1969

Write a ✓ next to the event that happened first.
☑ The Apollo 11 spacecraft launched from Earth.
☐ Armstrong and Aldrin landed a part of their spacecraft on the moon.

Write a ✓ next to the event that happened last.
☐ The astronauts collected moon soil.
☑ The astronauts returned to Earth.

On what date did the Apollo 11 spacecraft launch into space?
July 16, 1969

Who took the first steps on the moon?
Neil Armstrong

How many astronauts walked on the moon on July 21, 1969?
two

What did the astronauts bring back from the moon?
moon soil

The timeline on pages 98 and 99 tells about an event: the first moon landing. Stories can also tell about events. Stories can be about your life—events that were happy, important, silly, or more. Everyone has stories to tell!

Write about and draw the first thing you did today.
Where were you? **Answers will vary.**
How did you feel? **Answers will vary.**

Write about and draw a time you ate a food that surprised you.
What did you say? **Answers will vary.**

Write about and draw a time you and your family laughed.
What did it sound like? **Answers will vary.**

Write about and draw a time you want somewhere new.

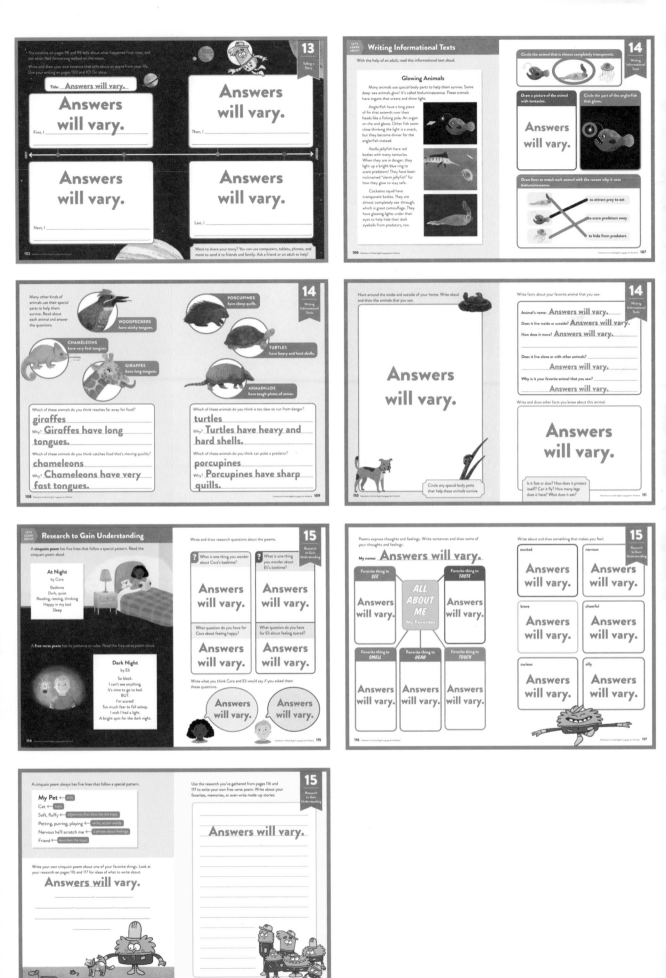

Odd Dot
120 Broadway
New York, NY 10271
OddDot.com

ISBN 978-1-250-31866-4

WRITER   Megan Hewes Butler

ILLUSTRATOR   Taryn Johnson

EDUCATIONAL CONSULTANT   Mindy Yip

CHARACTER DESIGNER   Anna-Maria Jung

COVER ILLUSTRATOR   Anna-Maria Jung

BACK COVER ILLUSTRATION   Chad Thomas

BADGE EMBROIDERER   El Patcha

LEAD SERIES DESIGNER   Carolyn Bahar

INTERIOR DESIGNERS   Carolyn Bahar and Abby Dening

COVER DESIGNERS   Carolyn Bahar and Colleen AF Venable

EDITOR   Nathalie Le Du

Our books may be purchased in bulk for promotional, educational, or business use. Please contact your local bookseller or the Macmillan Corporate and Premium Sales Department at (800) 221-7945 ext. 5442 or by email at MacmillanSpecialMarkets@macmillan.com.

DISCLAIMER
The publisher and authors disclaim responsibility for any loss, injury, or damages that may result from a reader engaging in the activities described in this book.

TinkerActive is a trademark of Odd Dot.
Printed in China by Hung Hing Off-set Printing Co. Ltd., Heshan City, Guangdong Province
First edition, 2019

10 9 8 7 6 5 4 3 2 1

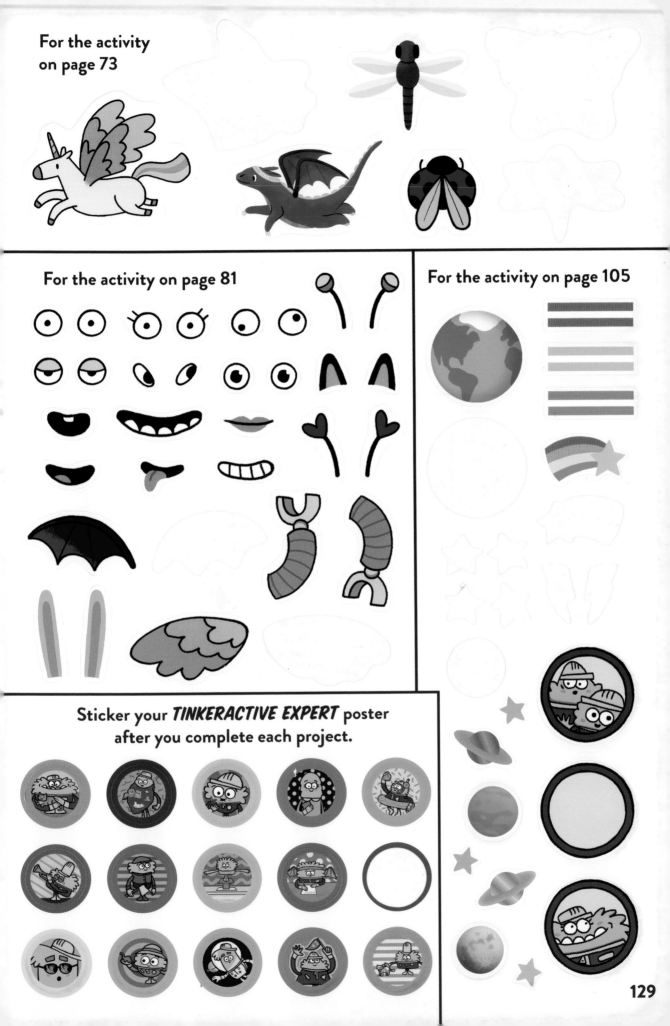

For the activity on page 73

For the activity on page 81

For the activity on page 105

Sticker your *TINKERACTIVE EXPERT* poster after you complete each project.